THE
MONEY
GARDEN

THE
MONEY
GARDEN

*How to Plant the Seeds
for a Lifetime of Income*

JULIE AUSTIN

CASTLE LAKE
PUBLISHING

The Money Garden
Copyright© 2009 Julie Austin
Published by Castle Lake Publishing
www.createforcash.com

Print edition:

ISBN 10: 0615328997
ISBN 13: 978-0615328997

Cover image: composite of iStockphoto©skodonnell, iStockphoto©Zemdega, and iStockphoto©Antagain. Photoshop by DesignForBooks.com.

Bookcover design and layout: DesignForBooks.com

Print edition, printed in the United States of America.

In memory of my grandmother, Mama Parney, who passed on her entrepreneurial genes to me.

Contents

Introduction

WHY I WROTE THIS BOOK AND
WHY YOU NEED TO READ IT

First of all, I want to tell you where I came from. I wasn't born rich and didn't have a lot of money growing up. But my parents sacrificed and made sure we never went hungry. We always had a roof over our heads and had plenty of love.

Before I was old enough to get a real job, I used to baby-sit and mow lawns for extra money. Then I discovered that I could collect cans, bottles, and newspapers, and cash those in for money. I felt like I was doing a good thing by recycling and cleaning up the neighborhood while fattening up my savings account at the same time. I found the best places for cans and bottles were at construction sites. The workers just threw them on the ground as trash, but for me that trash was cold, hard cash. They finally started boxing them up for me to pick up.

For me, as a little kid, every can and bottle represented a chance at a future. I was learning how to become an entrepreneur. And, without knowing it, I was putting together my first Money Garden.

Later, I figured out that I could use other skills to make money. I got several of my neighborhood friends together and started putting on talent shows. My dog Tinker was pretty cute, so I put him in there too. (I don't remember what his talent was. I think it was just looking cute.)

We had baton twirling, tap dancing, some singing, comedy sketches, and who knows what else. And we charged admission. I hate to think how awful it was. Maybe the neighbors just felt sorry for us, but I didn't care. I had paying customers and it was a business.

As I grew up, I lost the entreprenurial spirit for a while and started working for other people. In high school, I would go to classes in the morning and head straight to work at a movie theatre in the afternoon, eating my lunch in the car on the way. Then I would eat dinner in the car on the way to the mall, where I worked in a retail store. In my spare time and on the weekends I sold Avon door to door. Needless to say, I had little time to be a regular teenager.

When I turned eighteen, I packed my bags and headed for New York City. I didn't know a soul there and had actually never traveled to a big city before. I had a suitcase and a hundred dollars.

I had some vague idea that I was going to be a model, even though I was too short. I must have had a guardian angel looking over me in those first years, because I was just too young and naive to be living in New York City alone. To say that life was hard would be an understatement. A hundred dollars doesn't go very far in New York City.

I went from modeling agency to modeling agency and heard the same thing . . . "You're too short." But I didn't let that deter me. I went to every agency on my list and I finally found one that catered to shorter, commercial types. (By the way, I did actually end up getting on the covers of quite a few magazines.)

By sheer coincidence, I met a family the first day in that modeling agency that had also just moved to New York so that their daughter could pursue a modeling career. They asked me where I was living.

Well . . . I hadn't really thought about that. I guess I was just going to spend the small amount of money I had with me on a hotel room, and if I didn't get a job right away then . . . hmm . . . I don't know. I probably would have turned around and gone home. (Talk about not having a plan!)

The family I met asked me if I'd like to come live with them. It turns out that they were from the same town I was from and they were just as naive as I was. But they had an apartment. And they were really nice. So I went to live with them. I was in for a huge surprise, as the apartment was actually in the slums outside of the city. The floor used to be made of wood, but had been destroyed by termites or something and had disintegrated into dirt. It was what you call a "railroad" style apartment and the only door in the place was the bathroom door.

We didn't have much heat in the winter and there was no air conditioning in the summer. I had a bedroom, but it was so cold in the winter I would often sleep in the kitchen on a cot and turn on the oven to warm up the room. I would just pray that I didn't fall asleep with it on.

We also didn't have any hot water, and we didn't have a shower, the mother would boil water on the stove and pour it into the bathtub. This process took so long we would usually have to reuse the bathwater. I know . . . ick!

My bedroom was so tiny, it was just big enough for a bed. So I had to put nails into the wall and hang my clothes on them. Because it was so brutally cold, I usually just piled as many of the clothes as I could on top of the bed to keep warm. I was too naive to realize that I was living in a gang neighborhood. I didn't even know what a gang was. And many times the police would walk me home from the train station because it really wasn't safe to be out alone.

I lived this way for a couple of years, until one day I came home to the apartment and the landlord told me the family had left suddenly because the father was very ill. I never saw them again.

The landlord told me I had ten minutes to get my things and leave. When I walked in, the apartment was almost empty. I found a garbage bag and filled it with as many things as I could carry. I put on my warm hand-me-down coat and an old hat and sat on the front porch not knowing what to do or where to go.

I had a little bit of money and went to a local diner to get something to eat. I stood there in my old coat and hat with a garbage bag over my shoulder waiting to be seated. And I waited...and I waited. I finally realized that they thought I was a homeless bag lady, and they wouldn't seat me. I'll never forget that feeling. I ended up living in a fleabag hotel in the city until I could work and save enough money to get my own tiny apartment on the Upper Westside.

It took a long time to get back to being the entrepreneur I knew I always was. I resisted running my own company because I thought it was too much work, or too risky.

Too risky? Riskier than moving to New York City with a hundred dollars?

As for "too much work", to tell you the truth, work is all relative. If you really enjoy what you do, is it still considered work? I now think that working for other people is the real work. Most of what I do is play, and I get paid for it. These days having a job is what's really risky. There's no such thing as job security anymore, and starting a business isn't as risky as it used to be. There are ways to test a business with very little money or risk.

For more years than I want to count, I've been on a huge learning curve. And I've made many, many mistakes. But it's only through making so many mistakes that I've come to the point that I'm at now. I happen to think that making mistakes can be a very good learning tool. Not that I actively set out to make them. But by taking risks and just jumping in and doing it, I've learned about business from the bottom up.

I built my business up and crashed it down just as hard. Then I had to completely start over from scratch and build it back up again. There's something about dying and being reborn again that I've heard about from almost all entrepreneurs. I know ones who have been through bankruptcy, divorce, and devastating lawsuits. But they all survived and came back even stronger. They learned from their mistakes and used what they learned to grow their businesses even bigger and stronger than they were before.

I've distilled all that I've learned into this book so you don't have to go through what I went through. Is it valuable? You bet! That doesn't mean you won't have to put the work in, because you will. But now you will have a guide to keep you on track. I had to learn the hard way. (Boy, did I learn the hard way.) But that's how I know what I'm talking about—by living it.

Will you succeed if you actually go out and do what's in this book? Yes! Probably even beyond your wildest dreams. Is everyone going to go out and do it? Not likely.

Sometimes I tend to lump people into two categories, like pioneers and sheep, or doers and talkers. I can teach you to be an entrepreneur, but if you don't have the spirit, all you'll do is talk about it. If you're not committed to being a doer, you'll always just be a talker.

I wrote this book because, even though some people are born with a natural ability to be an entrepreneur, I still think it can be taught. What can't be taught is the "fire in the belly" determination. The ability to get up over and over and over again when you get knocked down. To start over as many times as it takes to succeed.

True entrepreneurs live life on the edge. But they also know that if they fall over, some how, some way, on the way down, they'll figure out how to make a parachute, cushion the blow, or grab onto the cliff. And even if they hit the ground, they'll just dust themselves off and climb back up again.

It took Thomas Edison about 20,000 failures before he came up with the version of the lightbulb that worked. That's what I'd call persistence!

So—what else does it take to be an entrepreneur?

One of the most important things you must have is passion. Passion for business and passion for life in general. Without it you'll never weather the intense storms, and incredible highs and lows of being an entrepreneur. No matter how many times you get knocked down (and you will), you need to be able to sustain that passion. Sometimes it's the only thing that will get you out of bed in the morning.

You have to look at challenges as opportunities. If you only see problems, you're likely to give up. It's all in the way you can turn things around and learn from them.

You really, truly have to love what you do. And the better you get at it, the more you'll love it. The more challenges you set up for yourself that you are able to meet, the more chances you'll take, and the more confident you'll be in your abilities. There will come a time when you'll start to believe that nothing is impossible.

Let everyone know what you're doing and your progress. They'll start to hold you accountable and you won't want to let them down. Don't let them down. Don't let yourself down.

Most people don't become entrepreneurs because they're afraid of failing. I hate to tell you, but if you are then you'll never make it. You have to have a tiny voice in the back of your head that says "Failure is not an option."

The best way to become an entrepreneur is to just get out there and do it. No matter what, you're going to make mistakes. Just try to keep them to a minimum and don't repeat the same mistakes. Learn from them. Believe it or not, failure is your best teacher. And you will always be learning. Never assume you know everything and keep your eyes open for people who can teach you. You can almost always learn something from everyone, even if you learn from their mistakes.

So many people I've talked to give one excuse after another for why they can't start a business yet. Too risky. No money. No time. Takes too long. I'm too old. I can't sell. I don't have enough confidence in my abilities. Blah, blah, blah.

Let's take a look at some of these excuses:

- **Too risky?** Risk comes with the job of being an entrepreneur—but so does reward. And the more you risk, the more chances you'll have to be rewarded. Like any game, the only way to win is to play. You'll never reach your dreams sitting on the sidelines.

- **Don't have any money?** Guess what, unless you get really lucky and find someone to give you gobs of money with no attachments, you'll *never* have enough to start. I never, ever found anyone to loan me money or invest in my company when I started out. You just have to find a way. Start small and bootstrap your business. Do what I did and work two or three jobs—whatever it takes. Don't worry, it's not forever. You just need enough to get started.

- **Don't have any time?** If you're working another job, then keep working it. Start your business after hours or on the weekends. You'll minimize your risk while you still have money coming in. You can always jump ship if you want when your business takes off.

- **Takes too long?** How long do doctors spend in medical school? How much time do attorneys invest in their careers? Olympic athletes? If you want to be a successful entrepreneur, you have to be willing to put in the time. The good news is that you can start earning some money at your business while you're building it. The same can't be said for doctors and lawyers.

- **Think you're too old?** Colonel Sanders was sixty-five when he franchised Kentucky Fried Chicken. And Michelangelo painted the Sistine Chapel when he was in his seventies. You're also never too young to start. I was only twelve when I started my recycling business.

- **Can't sell?** Selling is the number one basic skill of all entrepreneurs. If you need practice, get a weekend sales job. Try several different types of selling. Commission-only jobs force you to hone your skills, and it's going to be one of the most important skills you need to learn. And it can be learned. I worked several jobs where I made cold calls, and it helped prepare me for making calls for my own business.

- **Don't have confidence in your own abilities?** Once you start mastering the craft of being an entrepreneur you'll develop it. You will improve. And, don't be afraid to *ask* for what you want. You'll probably get a million "no's", but you have to keep asking. Somebody will say "yes". Just remember that for every seller, there's a buyer. Take that and build on it. Nobody likes to be the first to do anything. But once a product or business catches on and is "validated", then everybody wants in on it.

There will be many times when the only person that believes in you is *you*. Friends and family may try to be supportive, but if days turn into weeks, and weeks turn into years, and your business still hasn't taken off, you have to believe in it even more and stick with it.

In the beginning you may be just getting by. But the love of what you're building and what you're going to accomplish will keep you going. This is why entrepreneurs work unusually long hours.

For years I worked twelve hour days. (Oh, wait . . . I still do that.) If you love what you're doing, you'll want to spend more time doing it. (Have you ever noticed how much energy entrepreneurs have?) And you're working to make yourself rich, not some big corporation, so whatever you put into it is what you get out of it.

This also means only working with people who have a positive attitude. That's one of the benefits of being your own boss. Most of the time you get to pick who you want to spend time with. I turn down business all the time with people who are a pain in the butt. 'Cause guess what . . . they don't get any better. If they want to pay you too little and ask for too much, you can bet that it will be a never-ending nightmare.

If you want to be an entrepreneur, but are still holding on to the steady paycheck, then do it part-time until you're able to make the leap. While you're working a regular job, start saving your money, and make sure you have at least twelve months of living expenses, plus some extra savings to begin bootstrapping your business.

Always be planning for the business you'd like to start, because you may not have the final decision on when your job ends.

I was working at a job I hated (giving out movie passes) and making very little money. But I clung to it for years, afraid of making the leap to running my business full-time. I ended up getting fired because I got booked on a phone commercial and couldn't go into work that day. In the commercial, I was on a payphone actually calling my boss to tell him that I wouldn't be in that day. Since you couldn't hear my voice on the commercial, it didn't matter what I said. But I had to look happy on camera, even though I was being fired. Inside I was devastated. Devastated about losing a crappy job that I hated *and* that didn't pay very well.

So, I was forced to take the leap and I ended up with one of my first businesses . . . script reading. It was something I enjoyed, and I could do it part-time while getting my next business off the ground.

At this point, you might want to ask yourself why you want to be an entrepreneur. For me, the answer is very simple . . . freedom. I'm a doer. I like the feeling of never having to wait for people to get something done. If I want to start a project, I don't have to sit around a boardroom with a bunch of people trying to make a decision that takes months. And I don't have to explain why I'm buying inventory in nine colors or which ad I'm going to use. I don't have to listen to all of the reasons why something won't work. I just simply do it. If it doesn't work, I only have myself to blame. And then I'll just try something else until I figure out what *does* work.

And, with the Money Garden system I will never, ever get bored. There is always something to do, new lessons to be learned, new people to meet, and new projects to add to the "garden".

Years ago my dad had a great job with a major corporation. He had been there twenty-five years. At the time, I was struggling to form a company around a product I invented called swiggies, the wrist water bottle. I was constantly worried about whether I could pay the rent and buy groceries, while my dad got his weekly paycheck like clockwork. He told me I should just get a real job.

Flash forward to the present. My dad's "real" job at said major corporation was ending. He was asked to take early retirement, and left with little more than the contents of his desk. Meanwhile, I was making a comfortable living with swiggies and my script reading business.

Then it dawned on me that if I could keep two businesses going, I could keep ten going. And if I ever lost even half of them, I would still be making a great living.

So, I came up with a system that would have me juggling more plates than I ever imagined possible. Once I figured it out, it seemed easy. But after interviewing a wide range of people, I came to the conclusion that not everybody could figure it out on their own. That's why I wrote this book.

So many, like my dad, feel that security comes from a steady paycheck. But there's no such thing as job security anymore. The only people who will stay ahead of the curve will be the ones who create new and unique systems to make money.

I looked up the word 'job' in the dictionary. "A specific task done as part of the routine of one's occupation for an agreed price". "Anything a person is expected or obliged to do." "A difficult or strenuous task." Doesn't sound like fun, does it?

If all your income comes from one job, you're like a farmer with only one crop. If something goes wrong and the crop is wiped out . . . so are you.

I never liked the idea of betting the farm on just one crop, so I planted many of them. Different crops, in different fields, different markets, different countries, different weather, and with different people. If frost killed off one crop, I had others that thrived in the cold. If one was drowning in water, there were ones around it that flourished. I decided that I would never, ever be without a job because I would just keep creating more. At any given time, at least half of my "jobs" are making money. And I never have the fear of being laid off.

The purpose of this book is to give you the tools to create your own mini conglomerate. Your own mini empire of businesses that will eventually run themselves.

If you doubt that it will work, let's do some crazy math for a minute. Let's assume that you only sell one product and you make a whopping one dollar profit on it. Now, let's assume that you sell your product to 5% of the population of the United States.

As of this writing, the U.S. population is 305, 584, 500. That would mean a profit of $15, 279, 226. (305, 584, 500 x 5% = 15, 279, 226 people x $1.00/per person)

Pretty good, huh? Okay, let's assume only 1% of the U.S. population buys your product. That would be $3, 055, 845.

Still not a bad deal for selling one little product. But, because of the Internet, it's possible to sell all over the world easier and faster than ever before.

The world population, as of this writing, was $6,752,769,106$. Let's assume you only sell your product to 1% of the world population. That's a profit of $67,527,691.

Now, imagine if you had a whole money garden full of things to sell. That multiplies your chances, and those numbers will increase.

By the way, if you want to watch something interesting, go to www.census.gov and click on the population clocks. Watch to see how many babies are born every few seconds in the world. Those are your future customers!

Since I like keeping things simple myself, this book is very easy to understand and to implement. I've created my own Money Garden from the ground up with absolutely no money and no experience. When I started, I had no idea how to do it. I just figured it out through trial and error. But you can take the "error" out of it and try it for yourself using my guidance and knowledge. You'll be getting a shortcut to success that I had to learn the hard way.

Check out **www. createforcash.com** for ongoing articles and resources.

This book is a way for you to discover what took me years to learn:

That the world is full of endless possibilities . . . You just need to know how to harvest them.

1

Finding the Seeds to Plant

"Our aspirations are our possibilities"
—ROBERT BROWNING

"Exactly where do I find those endless possibilities?" you might be asking. They are literally everywhere. But the first thing I want you to do is to take a personal inventory. No, not how many cars or pairs of shoes you own. An inventory of your life experience. Because what you already know is far more valuable than you can imagine.

Are you a great mother? The best fund raiser in your church? Did you throw the best parties in college? Can you reassemble a car engine with your eyes closed? Have you climbed Mt. Everest? Do you make the best pumpkin pie in the whole world? Do you have the secret to making a relationship last?

Everyone is good at something. And if you dig deep enough, you'll find that you are good at many things.

Start when you were a kid:

- Did you have a newspaper route?
- A lemonade stand?
- Did you babysit?
- Collect cans and bottles?
- Mow grass?

When you were a teenager:

- Did you work at a fast food restaurant?
- Retail store?
- Bag groceries?
- Walk dogs?
- Sell Avon?

Jobs you did in college:

- Did you ever tend bar?
- Wait tables?
- Tutor kids?

What about after college? If you didn't go to college, what did you do instead? Take a look at your resume. How many jobs have you had through the years? Which jobs did you enjoy? In which ones did you really shine?

Do you tend to have creative skills, service and social skills, or do you have labor and craft skills?

If you have creative skills you will probably have the following traits:

- Observant
- Prolific
- Curious
- Puzzle solver
- Optimistic
- Persistent
- Flexible
- Risk taker

If you have labor and craft skills you probably:

- Like to repair things
- Are good with your hands
- Like to take things apart

If you have service and social skills you probably:

- Like helping others
- Like meeting new people
- Are good at talking to strangers
- Are empathetic to the needs of others

Look through the following checklist of skills and check off those you feel are your strengths:

WORKING WITH PEOPLE/COMMUNICATION

Entertaining, amusing or inspiring others

- ☐ Motivating or selling to others
- ☐ Establishing a level of rapport
- ☐ Advising or empowering others
- ☐ Working well with others as a team
- ☐ Communicating clearly to others
- ☐ Developing trust and confidence with customers and business clients
- ☐ Dealing with conflict situations
- ☐ Diagnosing, treating and healing others
- ☐ Negotiating with others to achieve goals
- ☐ Building and maintaining relationships

People Management:

- ☐ Holding people accountable
- ☐ Committing to the development of your employees
- ☐ Correctly evaluating the potential in others
- ☐ Rewarding achievement
- ☐ Encouraging others
- ☐ Clearly asking what you expect from others

Strategic Management:

- ☐ Assessing risk of decisions
- ☐ Adapting to change
- ☐ Seeing the big picture
- ☐ Understanding markets and customers
- ☐ Clearly seeing a vision for the future

Personal Characteristics:

- ☐ Showing confidence

- ☐ Listening to new ideas
- ☐ Thinking outside the box
- ☐ Listening and empathizing with the feelings of others

Managing Results:

- ☐ Producing good results
- ☐ Adapting to new technology
- ☐ Prioritizing
- ☐ Planning sales activities
- ☐ Showing good customer service
- ☐ Handling a crisis
- ☐ Working with complex documents
- ☐ Working well in a changing environment
- ☐ Solving problems creatively
- ☐ Implementing a step by step plan
- ☐ Managing budgets
- ☐ Breaking down a project so it can be put into action

Technical Skills:

- ☐ Making and producing things
- ☐ Cutting, carving, or chiseling
- ☐ Weaving or sewing
- ☐ Hand to eye coordination
- ☐ Working with precision tools
- ☐ Painting and restoring
- ☐ Building structures
- ☐ Growing things
- ☐ Operating equipment
- ☐ Raising or training animals
- ☐ Washing and cleaning
- ☐ Printing
- ☐ Working on computers

Creative or artistic skills:

- ☐ Sculpting or shaping
- ☐ Drawing or painting
- ☐ Web design
- ☐ Writing
- ☐ Graphic design
- ☐ Composing music
- ☐ Developing software

Working with Information:

- ☐ Writing business plans
- ☐ Writing grant proposals
- ☐ Implementing policies and procedures
- ☐ Evaluating risk management plans
- ☐ Keeping and managing records
- ☐ Breaking down and analyzing information

- ☐ Putting together research through interviewing or observing

Teaching Skills:

- ☐ Communicating effectively
- ☐ Developing and writing study courses
- ☐ Formulating clear objectives
- ☐ Encouraging and motivating students
- ☐ Giving good, valuable feedback
- ☐ Keeping up with current theories
- ☐ Using creative material
- ☐ Developing trust and confidence in students

If you're reading this book you probably already have some of the traits you need to manage your own Money Garden. Some of those are:

☐ Being and staying motivated
☐ Not afraid to make tough decisions
☐ Able to take charge and be a leader
☐ Independent thinker
☐ Able to turn problems into challenges

Something to consider when choosing your first business venture is the enormous amount of time you will be working in it. Even though I'm my own boss I never take a day off. If I do, I'll have to work harder the next day to catch up.

As I've said earlier, if you don't pick something you really love to do, you'll most likely quit because of the hours you'll have to work in the beginning to get your businesses off the ground. If you love what you do you'll be motivated to keep going for as long as it takes.

As an entrepreneur you will always have to make tough decisions. In the beginning those decisions will be different from the ones you make further down the road, like when you start hiring and firing employees. You'll also have to make a lot of tough decisions about money and where to spend it.

In the beginning, unless you have a partner, you'll be all alone. You will be the boss. The benefit to being an employee is that you don't have to make those hard decisions. When your day is over you can go home and relax. When you're the boss you will always have the business on your mind. The entrepreneur's brain will never rest.

You'll have to get used to being a leader, delegating to others, and learning how to turn problems into solutions. You have to make things work no matter what. When I got to the point that I realized other people really depended on me, it was a bit scary. You have to be able to manage other people and take charge.

Today 70% of the workforce is in the service sector. Since your first business will very likely be a service business (you already know how to do it and it's cheap and easy to start), look through your resume for a creative, labor, or social job that you can turn into a business. Then review your skills, talents, and interests for even more ideas. You can also look through the yellow pages to see service businesses others have started that might be logical fits for your talents.

Here is a list to get you thinking:

WHAT KIND OF BUSINESS WOULD YOU LIKE TO HAVE?

☐ Are you an early riser or do you get more creative late at night?

☐ Do you like working indoors or outdoors?

☐ Do you like working alone or with a partner?

☐ Do you like to travel?

☐ Do you want to manage employees or have assistants?

☐ Do you have book smarts or street smarts?

☐ Are you prepared to work very long hours in the beginning managing all aspects of the business?

Gift Baskets

If you're artistically inclined, gift baskets might be a good business for you. It's a year-round business, but especially profitable during the holidays.

Antique Restoration Service

This is a good labor-intensive business if you like to restore, repair, and refinish collectibles, cars, and antique furniture. You'll need to have a knowledge of old and new wood finishing techniques for furniture, and knowledge of auto repair and other skills for classic car restoration. This business could branch out to combine with being a collectible middleman, an antique dealer, or to renting out your own antique cars to the film industry.

Income Tax Preparation Service

The only thing that's certain is death and taxes. So until that changes, everybody needs to get their taxes done. Most people who start this kind of business have a degree in accounting and have had some on the job experience. Even though there's work to do all year long, it's more of a seasonal job.

Massage Therapy

There are over a hundred and fifty different types of massage practiced today. And there will always be stressed out people. Certifications vary from state to state, but typical training programs are between five hundred and a thousand hours. Massage therapy is a great part or full time business or it could be expanded to a full spa business.

Tour Service

If you live in an area that's either historical or unique you could start a tour service. It could be a bus or van tour, or it could be a walking tour. Go off the beaten track from the typical tourist areas and offer something unique and different. Find facts and locations that you wouldn't find in the standard guidebook for that area.

Photography

Many photographers specialize in either people, pets, or events. It's a good idea to have a niche market, like shooting weddings or children or fashion. Some photographers specialize in real estate photography or in product photography. You'll need a good camera, lenses, and lighting, along with some training. (Most community colleges have inexpensive courses in photography.)

Transcription Service

If you're a fast typist and understand technical terms, you will probably do well with a transcription business. Transcription machines have been replaced by CDs that you play in your computer while you listen to the audio via headphones. You'll need a digital transcription software program, and of course, a computer. You can find a lot of work through doctors and lawyers.

Cleaning Service

This is a business you can start yourself, and eventually hire employees to help you. You don't need a lot of skills, just a willingness to work hard and get your hands dirty. There are only so many hours you can work each day by yourself and employee turnover is high. You and your employees should both be bonded. You can work for private residences, schools, hospitals, or retail establishments. You can also specialize in specific areas like carpet or window cleaning.

Alterations

If you already do your own sewing you'll have most of the skills and tools you need to do alterations. This is a business you can run from home so you save money on a shop. Contact business organizations to get started and offer a discount for their employees if the business will let you put flyers in the reception area to attract new business.

Tutoring Service

If you're an expert in a particular subject, you might look into tutoring. You should be good at transferring knowledge in a way that the student will understand. Having a passion or at least a strong interest in the subject is helpful. Check to see if your state requires a license or certification.

Property Manager

This is a business you can start even if you don't have a home. You'll be responsible for screening the tenants, collecting rents, keeping the building clean and safe, and either fixing or having things fixed when they break. Some property managers have to be bonded, and certainly need to be trustworthy. You might even be able to work a non-competing home business during your off hours.

Pet Grooming

It's a given that you must love pets. And you should have some training at a pet grooming salon for at least several months before venturing out on your own. You can work from home or have a mobile grooming service that goes to your customers. You'll need tools like clippers and trimmers, and supplies like shampoo and flea powder. Practice on your own or your neighbor's pets.

Handyman Service

You don't have to be a man, just skilled at fixing things. You'll be doing minor jobs like fixing a leaky faucet, replacing windows, or repairing a cabinet door. Calling a professional plumber or electrician for small jobs can get expensive. And a handyman can do just as good of a job. You can work on your own or through property managers. You'll need to be licensed and insured, and have your own tools. And the more you know, the more you'll earn. So keep learning.

Sales Rep

If you want a business that doesn't have any start-up costs, and you have unlimited energy and enthusiasm, a sales rep business may be perfect for you. Most sales reps work for manufacturers or wholesalers, and some have territories they service. They may sell one product or rep several lines from different manufacturers. Usually they work on a commission basis and can make anywhere from 2% to 35% depending on the product and the amount of work involved.

Child Care Service

If you want to run a child care business you really must love kids. Usually home-based child-care services take care of four to six children. Some could be full daycare and some might be part-time. You'll be responsible for their care, meals, snacks, nap time, and activities. You'll need to be licensed and certified, and have plenty of room to take care of the children. If you're serving food, you'll need additional licensing and certification. You should also have plenty of toys and games to keep the children busy.

PUT IT INTO ACTION

- ☐ Make a list of five of your best skills
- ☐ Write down your number one God-given talent
- ☐ List your creative, social, and labor skills
- ☐ Pick out the area where you have the most skills
- ☐ Ask several people who know you well what talents they feel are your strongest
- ☐ Look through your resume and find one job skill that you could turn into a business
- ☐ Write down everything you have been in charge of
- ☐ Write down your ideal daily schedule
- ☐ Do some research on a service business, which matches up well with your experience and abilities

2

Finding the Right Plot of Land

*"Diamonds are nothing more than
chunks of coal that stuck to their jobs"*
—MALCOLM FORBES

We've already taken an inventory of your experiences and skills, now let's build on that by adding the things that you like to do. Do you like playing golf? Watching TV? Reading? Traveling? If you had all the money you would ever need in the bank, how would you spend your time? What do you enjoy and what do you know the most about?

This will help you come up with the topics for your businesses, i.e. photography, jewelry, cooking, landscaping, etc. You can have as many as you want. And the list may grow through the years. (Later on I'll show you how to link different businesses together for maximum effectiveness.) You'll want to match your best skills with the things you really like to do. You're going to be working long hours, but if it's fun it won't seem like work. It won't seem like a J...O...B.

Nikola Tesla, the famous inventor, worked from ten in the morning until five the next morning, seven days a week. This was a man who loved his "job"!

And trust me, once you get the system working, the energy will feed on itself. You'll wonder why you didn't do it sooner.

I think people make things much more complicated than they need to be. If this system was something that was too complicated, I wouldn't be teaching it to you. I certainly wouldn't be preaching it with absolute enthusiasm, and telling you that if you do everything in this book, you'll not only make a lot of money, you'll have a better quality of life, if I didn't believe it. I'm not saying you'll make a million dollars or rule the world. Maybe you will, but you will at least make enough money to enjoy a good life and do what you *want* to do.

It should only take a few months to get up and running with a steady income. But the system is a work in progress, and the whole thing could take years. You just keep adding on to it, like a giant snowball rolling down the mountain. The great thing is, the sky's the limit. You get out of it what you put into it.

I want you to get into the habit of writing everything down. First of all, your memory will never be as good as you think it is. And by the time you finish reading this book, you will be thinking faster than you can write.

Also, there's just something about putting an idea down on paper that helps you come up with more ideas to add on to it. So have pen and paper everywhere. In your car. Next to your bed. In your purse. You never know when an idea will hit you. And once you start looking for ideas you will find them everywhere.

I have whiteboards covering all of the walls of my office. One actually says "Ideas Galore". Every time I have an idea I add to it. There are many that I had forgotten about that just needed to be dusted off and worked on. List everything. You never know how valuable an idea could be or when the timing is right to launch it.

Once you come up with your topics, start keeping folders for each topic and gather information to put in them. By now you should have that giant list of "things you're good at" and "things you like to do". Now you want to narrow it down to a few topics.

I currently have five topics:

- Entrepreneurship
- Running
- Inventions
- Movies
- PR

Now you want to start creating mind maps for each topic. For centuries, mind mapping has been used by psychologists, engineers, teachers, and inventors as a form of brainstorming and visual problem solving. It helps you expand and develop ideas and link them together in ways you might not otherwise.

Visionary Tony Buzan created the modern day version of the mind map, which uses words, images, numbers, and colors to expand the potential of the brain. By laying every-

---

BUSINESS TOPICS

Here are a few examples of topics to get you thinking:

Relationships	Writing	Spa Industry
Computers	Medicine	Cleaning
Family	Fashion	Landscaping
Cars	Motorcycles	Fishing
Animals	Sports	Holidays
Food	Childcare	History
Dance	Teaching	Art
Fitness	Entertainment	Cosmetics
Real Estate	Investments	Vitamins
Games	Law	Jewelry
Music	Golf	Tattoos
Travel	Carpentry	Stamps & Coins
Crafts	Floral Design	Stained Glass

---

thing out in this visual form, it helps you to see the big picture and avoid linear thinking.

So what exactly is a mind map and how do you make one? A mind map lays out all of your ideas in a series of circles so that you can see how your ideas link to each other and how you can create more ideas by interconnecting them.

Start with a circle in the middle of the page. Put one of your topics in it, like the example below:

Running

Then start branching out with more circles that relate to that topic, like below:

Then you can start adding more topics and figure out ways to link the topics together, like this:

Running

Inventions for runners (my own & other people's

Do PR for runners— sponsor runners

Inventions

PR

Do PR for inventors

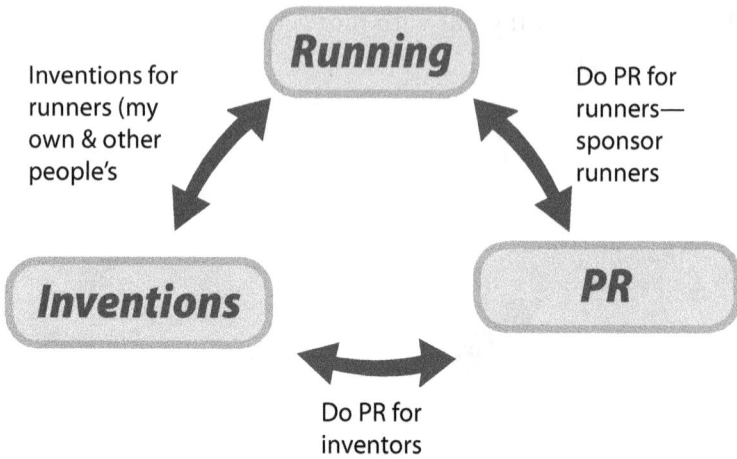

When I get involved in a new project I put everything down on paper and whiteboards. Then I spread everything out on the floor around me so I can see it all at once. Some of it is mind maps and some is just random notes and research. But I like to spread it out like a puzzle that I'm piecing together.

A good way to become more prolific is to write different topics on different sections of whiteboard and start filling them in. This is how you can avoid getting stuck with writer's block. When you run out of ideas for one, start on another.

From now on all of your ideas should be put down on paper. Mind mapping is a powerful way to visualize your future. Once you're able to see what it looks like, you know what needs to be done. Mind maps also help you to structure and generate ideas, and it's a way to hold yourself accountable. Put it down on paper and make it happen.

"THE SYSTEM"

The System takes your topics, skills, and delivery methods and links them together. Once you learn how to put together one system, you can start another one and another one. Create a template and start dropping things in it. The more advanced you get, the more systems you'll create and the more you'll be able to link together. Kind of like mini universes that create one big solar system, with you at the center.

Another way to think about the Money Garden System is like a portfolio. You always hear that you should diversify. A Money Garden is a diversified portfolio of businesses. You should have products, services, events, and intellectual property. These should be seasonal and non-seasonal, high, medium and low end products and services, and diversified in different topics for maximum effect. Even better if you have products for all age groups.

Once you get the broad topics you can start branching out into subtopics. The whole trick of this is to come up with as many businesses as you can that will all eventually run themselves. You'll just be the ringleader. You want to create as many income sources as possible under as many topics as possible.

PYRAMIDING UP

When I started my first business I had less than no money. I was actually in debt. So I had to learn to do everything without money, which can be a blessing and a curse. I made my first prototype for swiggies out of clay. I worked two jobs and saved up enough money a little at a time to do everything piecemeal.

Once I had the actual product manufactured, I started by having it made in the U.S. I couldn't even afford to have the factory assemble them, so I assembled them all myself in my living room. By the end of the day my fingers were bleeding.

I had a thousand sets of swiggies (at the time they were called HydroSports) in my apartment. But I didn't have any packaging for them. So I went to a friend who had a manufacturing plant and he gave me a few hundred plastic packages to put the product in. After putting together a header card and getting a UPC code, I now had a workable product.

The reason I bring this up is that, even if you don't have money to work with, just start wherever you can and pyramid up. By bootstrapping your business you will only use the money you earn in profit and not overextend yourself with loans. And you'll learn how to use money *very* wisely. If you can't afford it, you'll have to figure out another way to do it. This is how guerilla marketers are born.

By not being able to hire people, you'll learn the business from the ground up. You'll know how to do every job. This includes hauling boxes and making your own sales calls. Learning to sell is a skill that will come in very handy, since in almost all businesses you're always selling.

Even though I barely knew what I was doing, naively, I contacted the buyer of a local chain of sporting good stores, and got the product in all of their stores. I sold the whole lot of swiggies. Then I took the profit I made and invested in more inventory. This time I doubled it. Then I took the new inventory and sold that and bought more. Each time I doubled my inventory, and took the profit to do more marketing, which resulted in more sales and more money to keep pyramiding up.

Do the same thing with your advertising. Spend a small amount of money to place some Google Ads or classified ads. If you spend $25 and make $35 then you have made a profit. Okay, it's not a big profit. But take that $35 and invest in more and just keep going.

The more places you can get your business seen, the better. Always make sure your business is out there . . . somewhere. It has a cumulative effect.

Along the way I was learning the hard way about how to run a business. And even if you have money to start your business, I would still do it in this order:

- Marketing for free
- Marketing cheap
- Marketing with money

You'll find that the things you do for free to run your business will often be the ones that work the best. Do them even as your business grows. But as your business grows, you'll be able to spend some of your profits to grow your business even more. Incorporate all three and move on to the next business and start the process all over again while continuing to work on the first one.

Of course, there are many ways to start and finance a business. Personally, I was never able to get investors or bank loans, but I still think you should put together a marketing and business plan to help guide you. Many times investors won't come around until you are up and running and making a certain amount of money, but when that day comes, you'll be much better off if you have a marketing and business plan ready to show them.

Hopefully, you will get at least some of your businesses to the million dollar or multi-million dollar level. Then you might want to look into getting investors to push it over the edge or even take it public. By then you won't need to give away the same amount that you would if it was still a start-up.

I've found that most people don't want to help you until you have actually done as much work as possible first. Think about it. Investors want you to have some skin in the game. And most people want to see that you're working hard and you have passion for your business. Then people will step in to help. Take your business as far as you possibly can yourself. Pyramid it up!

THE MARKETING PLAN

A marketing plan is like a roadmap for a business. It helps to identify markets and measures the effectiveness in getting new customers. They are more informal than business plans and are written for internal use. Before starting a marketing plan you need to understand the market you are involved in. You should be studying where it's been, where it's going, and how you fit into it.

You'll want to know how companies before you have done business and whether you want to follow that strategy, or do something totally different. You need to factor in things such as the economy and government regulations. What's going on in the world will also affect your business.

Now that you have ideas for several businesses, here are some questions for you to ask yourself about each:

Is your business in any danger of being phased out?

Technology and innovation change the way we live and do business and it changes quickly.

Is your industry still going to be around in a few years?

You should be aware of trends and be able to figure out where your company fits into them.

Is your product or service a fad?

A popular fad today can disappear tomorrow.

Your marketing plan should include what makes your company different. What is your company's mission statement? What makes you different from the competition? Make sure you really know your competition and how you can differentiate yourself from them. What are they doing right? What are they doing wrong? What do your potential customers think about the competition?

Who is your target market? Instead of trying to sell to everyone, find out which group will be your best market and target your efforts towards them. Do your products or services satisfy a basic need, solve a problem, or satisfy an emotional need? Consider your market's gender, age, income level, ethnic background, education, location, marital status, etc. Then do some research into their lifestyle; like their interests, hobbies, attitudes, and which social class they fit into.

Find out what your customer's needs are. Put together a customer profile and learn how you can tailor your products or services to fit their needs. Stay in touch with customers to see if their needs are changing. Maybe they want more or less of the product you're selling to them. Maybe they want more of a product line and extra benefits with the old ones.

Your marketing plan should include your distribution channels. Will you be primarily on the Internet or will you have a brick and mortar store? Will you market through catalogs, or affiliate programs, or both. How will orders be processed, billed and shipped? What kind of credit terms do you offer? What about your return policy? Does it come with a warranty?

Will you be using reps, distributors, phone sells, or product demonstrators? Will you use a sales training program? What are the key selling points of your product or service? Is it faster, more convenient, or easier to use than the competition? What's your "Unique Selling Proposition"?

You need to develop a pricing strategy for your company's products and services. This will be based on calculating your costs and comparing your products or services to existing ones. Make sure you calculate all of your costs; fixed and variable costs. Add in freight costs, labor and administrative costs.

Can you sell your products at a lower cost and still make money? How do you explain to the customer that you are able to sell it for less? If you sell it for more money will people still be willing to buy it?

You need to put in a section on advertising and publicity. Where will you advertise; the Internet, TV, newspapers, magazines, radio or direct mail? Part of the sales promotion you will do may include coupons, point of purchase displays, free samples, etc. If you don't have money to advertise, what will you do to promote awareness of your business?

Publicity should be included in your marketing plan. Either do it yourself or hire a PR firm to help with your product launches, special events, and press releases. Your marketing plan should be updated regularly as things change and you branch out into other markets.

THE BUSINESS PLAN

Your company should have a business plan even if you're not looking for investors. Like a marketing plan, a business plan is a roadmap that helps you determine your financial destination and prepares you for problems and opportunities that will come along in the future. You wouldn't set out on a cross-country trip without a map. Nor should you start a business without a map of where you're going and how you're going to get there.

Even if you don't plan to look for investors or bank loans now, you never know what you'll do in the future. You never know how well your business will do and if you will need to look for venture capital in the future.

Business plans should have key points, including an overview of the management team, a description of the company, information about the product or service you're selling,

Masterplans uses a team planning model to craft business plans for entrepreneurs. Here is some of their advice for the small business owner:

Do all businesses need a business plan?

Every business that wants to succeed should have a business plan. Not only will a well-written business plan greatly enhance your chances of long-term success, but it will also bring a focus and clarity to your project. This will allow you to accelerate the process in every facet of your business. A business plan can be used for multiple purposes: operational purposes, raising capital, internal strategy, and providing the business with a "roadmap". By its nature, it's a living, breathing document that will change and evolve with the business.

What goes in a typical business plan?

A comprehensive business plan would contain the following:

- **Executive summary**—An overview of the business, it's goals, the market, and key management. It also highlights the financial Pro Forma.
- **Product or service description**—A complete description of products or services being offered by your company.
- **Market and industry analysis**—A comprehensive analysis of the market and industry you're doing business in, including competitive and demographic research.
- **Financial projections (Pro Forma)**—A projected model of your company's financial future, including start-up costs, break-even analysis, cash flow, and profit and loss figures.
- **Investment proposal**—An investment ready business plan requires this component. This entails a valuation of your business model and a scheduled payback to the investor, including a well-defined exit strategy for the investor.

All business plans are different and unique, but the basic components listed above are always present.

Where would you suggest the entrepreneur take the plan?

To the appropriate funding source for their particular project, factoring profit or non-profit status, start-up or existing business, whether debt or equity financing is needed.

> **Debt** financing loans are primarily obtained through the bank or SBA.
> **Equity** financing can be obtained through private investors, including, but limited to angel investors or venture capital firms. Often times a combination of debt and equity financing is appropriate.
>
> ***Does a small business need a marketing plan and a business plan?***
>
> A comprehensive business plan will contain a marketing strategy with key initiatives as one of its components. When done properly, it will provide recommendations to implement targeted and proven methods to grow a particular business model. The marketing strategy is the "what" and the marketing plan is the "how". Typically the marketing plan is a separate document.

market analysis and strategies, and most important of all—the financials.

If you're just starting a small service business, creating a business plan may seem like overkill. But do it anyway because it will force you to think in detail about the future challenges you'll face.

Planning to Give

The era of greed is over and the ways we have been doing business are rapidly changing. What used to work doesn't work anymore and entrepreneurs are experimenting with the challenges of a new business model. One thing you'll start to find is that you now need to *give* to get. (Don't worry, it's a good thing. Doing good releases endorphins and strengthens the immune system.)

If you want people to go to your website, it helps to give them something. It could be free content, a valuable service, a free ebook, or connections to other people. You should constantly be increasing your network and giving to them as they also give to you. Good Samaritans always end up on the evening news. I'm sure I'm not the only person who sees a businessperson who really gives something extra to the customer and thinks "That's the kind of person I want working for me".

If giving sounds like a lot of work, you're right. But when you're doing what you love and helping others at the same time, when you can't wait to jump out of bed and start working, is it really work? The world is full of givers, but there are also plenty of people out there that are just takers. They only take and never give. If you find out you're dealing with a pure taker, cut them off quickly. This is somebody who's not a team player and they'll just suck your blood. Don't waste your time. Plug into the yin and yang of the universe and let it work for you. Surround yourself with team players that feed off of and transform each other.

Another way you can give is to offer others the chance to share in your profits through referrals. If you're not playing the referral game, you're missing out on one of the easiest and best streams of income. You could spend hundreds of dollars to take out an ad, and maybe you would end up with new customers and maybe you wouldn't. If you instead said to everyone you know, "Look, I'll give you 10% if you bring me a new client" you would know for sure that you're going to make money if they bring you someone. And it only costs you 10%. It's a win-win. On the other hand, you should also ask everyone you know if *you* could make 10% from them if you bring *them* a new client.

I know what you're think-
ing, "But, Julie, giving should be
unconditional". Yes . . . if you're
sponsoring a needy child or bringing your neighbor gifts in the hos-
pital, or adopting a puppy from the
shelter. But business is different.
Business owners know the value
of a customer who comes from a
qualified referral. People like to do
business with people they know,
like, and trust. So make sure you
really believe in the product, ser-

> ### Tip
>
> Every time you meet someone new, you should increase your chances for future referrals by doing the following:
>
> - Ask open-ended, feel-good questions to learn more about them
> - Ask them how you can help them
> - Promise to stay in touch, keep your word, and do it often

vice, or person you are recommending. If you believe in them
yourself, your enthusiasm will show through.

Since the average person knows about 250 people, and
each of those people knows 250 people, imagine how big that
potential network is. Start thinking of referrals as a win/win
situation that works both ways. When you refer other people,
you win money and they win good customers. When someone
refers business to you, you win customers and they win money.

Send holidays cards to your bigger customers. Send cards
for another holiday than just Christmas. Like maybe Easter or
Halloween. It'll be unexpected and won't get lost with all the
others. Send thank you cards whenever someone does something nice for you. People rarely do it, so it won't be expected,
but will be greatly appreciated.

Diversity

When farmers ready a plot of land, part of their planning includes how they will rotate their crops. Crop rotation is a system of growing certain crops on the same field. It means that the succeeding crops are of a different species or variety than the previous crops. This is to avoid the buildup of pests and pathogens that happens when one crop is grown continuously in the same field. It also helps to avoid depletion of the soil's nutrients. It improves the soil's structure by alternating plants with deep roots and ones with shallow roots. By using this system farmers can keep all of their fields in continuous production.

This is the same thing you need to do with your Money Garden. By having several different businesses, you can concentrate on the ones that are making the most money, and by having seasonal businesses you can focus heavily on the right one for the right season. If you sell sunscreen in the summer, have another product you can sell in the winter.

There are other factors to consider. The economy ebbs and flows. Some businesses will do better than others in a down economy. That's when you shift your focus to another business. Fads and pop culture affect sales of a product. What goes on in the world affects different businesses. So does the weather. Just like your financial portfolio, you need to be diversified with your businesses.

And you should also trim the weeds in your Money Garden. If something isn't working, change it. Test different advertising messages to see which ones appeal to your customers. Use split runs, or two different versions of an ad, to see which one is more effective. This can be done by using a specific code on a direct mail postcard or on a classified ad.

You can also do this with your website. Visitors to your site will see different sales pages. You can track which ones convert into sales and which ones don't. Test one component at a time for the best results. You can test short copy against long copy, different price points, headlines, or the design of the site.

The only way to find out what works and what doesn't is to just jump in and do it. Use tracking software to help you hone in on your best results.

PUT IT INTO ACTION

- ☐ Buy several pieces of white posterboard and a set of colored ink pens.
- ☐ Put your topics in the middle of each one and circle them.
- ☐ Put together your first Money Garden mind map.
- ☐ Buy several small notepads and pens and put them everywhere.
- ☐ Start putting together the basics for your marketing and business plan.
- ☐ Thank someone for helping you. Send them a card.

C H A P T E R

3

Creating Your Garden

"The best way to get a good idea is to get a lot of ideas"
—NOBEL PRIZE WINNER LINUS PAULING

It's been shown that people who like what they do tend to come up with more ideas. If you're going to become your own mini mogul, you're going to have to learn how to come up with tons of new ideas. Creativity is based on cognitive processes we all share. You just need to learn how to tap into them.

When you mention the topic of creativity, most people don't put a lot of value in it. They would equate it with writing poetry or with taking art classes at school. Not that poetry and art aren't valuable, but most people can't make a lot of money at them. The way we'll use creativity is in creating businesses that will make you money. We'll use creativity to stand out from the crowd and make your business more unique.

To get started, take each of your topics and put together a file for it. Accumulate research on every topic and immerse yourself in it. You need constant input on a daily basis. The more knowledge you accumulate, the more you can combine it with other ideas.

If you're going to come up with new ideas, you're going to have to shake up your daily routine. And you're going to have to absolutely force yourself to get out of your comfort zone. (No, sitting in another chair in the living room doesn't count.)

Force yourself to have a wide variety of life experiences. Get out and try new things. Take a different route to the store. Eat at a different restaurant. Meet different kinds of people. Listen to a different radio station. Watch a different channel on TV. Try a new recipe. Do at least one new thing every single day.

Go looking for ideas at museums, art galleries, lectures, flea markets, seminars, etc. Study history and come up with new twists on old ideas. Visit new cities or countries you've never seen before. You don't have to go far. Just get in your car and drive to a place you've never been to before. Take a tour of the city. This will put you in a new frame of mind, and open you up to new experiences. Many cities have haunted ghost tours, historical tours, and other unique ways to learn about the city's unusual features.

See the city from a different angle, like from the air, or from a boat. Become an explorer. Travel without a schedule or map. And keep notes of everything. You never know what might come in handy.

Make a point of talking to people you meet in your travels. Listen to their stories. They will be full of valuable information. Talk to people of different ages, and people from different cultures.

Also, in your travels, look to nature for inspiration. Sometimes, a particular pattern of a flower or a tree will spark an idea. Be curious, and always ask yourself why something is the way it is. Ask yourself a lot of questions and keep asking.

Look at something and imagine it as something else. This is a great way to come up with an endless amount of ideas. You are only limited by your imagination. Look up at the clouds and see how many different things you can see in them.

Another great way to come up with ideas is to watch TV with the sound off. It's a good way of looking at one thing and seeing something else. Go to your local library and walk up and down the aisles. Randomly pick up a book and start looking through it. You might be surprised at what you learn. Pick up a dictionary and randomly turn to a page. Try to link the first word you see to one of your topics. Do this every day. One day the two will combine to become a great new idea.

Look through the yellow pages for inspiration. What kind of niche business is missing? How can you take an existing business and come up with a better angle on it? Combine different words, tastes, smells, systems, etc. Keep combining until you hit the jackpot. Ask yourself "What if?" every day.

Maintain your child-like curiosity. Never get jaded or take things for granted. Having fun opens you up to being more creative. Fill your office with silly, goofy things that will put you in the right mood. Wear a crazy hat or wild, silly clothes. Get used to being different.

Children see everything as new and exciting, with no rules. They also ask way more questions than adults do. Always ask questions if you don't understand something. You're not stupid for not knowing the answer, but you'll be stupid if you don't ask the question.

Start looking at problems as a challenge instead of something negative. Tackle a crisis head-on and figure out what you can learn from it. Don't wallow in the pain, figure out how you can make it work for you.

Get out and interact with people. All kinds of people. Engage yourself in conversation with strangers. Have an intelligent, but civil, debate with someone. Stretch your brain. Learn how the other side thinks.

Take at least one risk every week. Do something completely different that you've never done before.

Pay attention to things and really, really see them. Notice three things in your room or in your neighborhood that you've never seen before. Look for these things every day. It'll force you to start looking at details.

Look to other fields for ideas. Look in fields you're not familiar with. Mix and match ideas you are familiar with. What ideas from History, Math, Science, or Biology can you use? How can you apply those ideas to something you're working on now?

Pay attention to unusual patterns. If you look around you right now I bet you'll see several that you never noticed before. Think of the end of one thing as the beginning of another.

Sit down at the computer and just start typing. I call this "opening doors". It's kind of a random, stream of consciousness exercise:

Start with a sentence and see where the last word leads you. For example, "I'm waking up with a hot cup of coffee in my special mug. Mug shots are police photographs of a suspect's face. Face the class when you are giving a speech." See how it works? Just keep going as fast as you can without stopping or editing yourself. When you're in your creative frame of mind, don't edit yourself. You can do that later.

Don't be afraid to make a fool out of yourself. Get in the habit of forcing yourself to do things you normally wouldn't do. Stretch your creative brain!

So . . . what's the purpose of this explosion of creative thinking activities all about? Why are you "stretching your brain"?

The goal is to get lots of information flowing in your mind so that you might link things together in a way that creates new products, marketing ideas, business concepts, and so on.

For example, let's say you take a trip to the beach and you walk along the surf. Your shoes get wet and full of water as the tide races under your feet. You start to think about the linkage between water and shoes. You think to yourself, "Hey, maybe they could make a shoe completely out of something waterproof, like rubber." As you start thinking about a rubber shoe, you realize that although the shoe itself would stay dry, it could still fill up with water. So, you decide to put holes in it to let the water drain out.

As you visualize what this slip on rubber shoe with holes in it might look like, you start to think it might be a little funny looking. Then you notice some kids walking along the beach, singing and skipping as they go.

Hmmm. Maybe this shoe could be sold to kids, since they don't seem to be very self-conscious and wouldn't care what other people would think. But—it would have to be in bright colors, since kids love bright colors.

You start to notice a few adults here and there wearing bright colors, or a goofy hat, or something else that not everyone would care for. Now you think that the adults who aren't very self-conscious are a possible market too, and they would probably like the bright colors as well.

You start thinking about which adults would be most concerned about getting their shoes wet. Probably not folks walking on the beach, as most would be barefoot. But boaters might be a logical group to start marketing to, and then things might spread from there.

If any of this sounds familiar, it's probably because you're thinking about the Crocs® shoe.

PUT IT INTO ACTION

- [ ] Drive down a street you've never been on before
- [ ] Listen to a radio station you've never listened to before
- [ ] Go to a museum with a notepad and make notes about the artwork
- [ ] Drive to a new city or town and sightsee
- [ ] Find a new recipe and cook it for dinner

CHAPTER

4

Finding the Right Fertilizer

"Life isn't about finding yourself, it's about creating yourself."
—GEORGE BERNARD SHAW

Fertilizer helps put the right ingredients in place for seeds to grow and sprout. In this chapter, I want to give you the knowledge you can put in place to enable your topics, and all the associated ideas you've generated, to sprout into businesses.

Your creations may include products, services, events, or combinations of those elements, but in any case, you'll be creating several cash crops to put into your mini-conglomerate. You'll also find that you'll be generating a lot of "intellectual property" as you develop new businesses.

The definition of intellectual property from Wikipedia states that it is "a legal field that refers to creations of the mind, such as musical, literary, and artistic works, inventions, and symbols, names, images, and designs used in commerce, including copyrights, trademarks, patents, and related rights".

Why is intellectual property so important? Because one or more of your businesses might be primarily based on intellectual property.

For example if one of your topics is "inventions", and you invent a new product (as I did for swiggies), then a patent might be a vital part of your business.

Or, if one of your topics is "writing", you might create books or ebooks in your areas of knowledge, in which case copyright protection would become very important to your operations.

Even if you don't have a business that depends on these kind of creative works directly, you'll still be generating materials you'll want to copyright (like the content of a website promoting your business) or trademark, like the unique name of your business or products.

Since you will definitely need at least some working knowledge of intellectual property, let's discuss the four main types: patents, copyrights, trademarks, and trade secrets.

PATENTS

You don't have to have a patent to sell a product. But having a patent does exclude others from selling the same product, and it gives you an instant competitive advantage. The patent gives your business a valuable asset. If you plan to license the product, you should also have a patent, or at least a patent pending (which means you have filed a patent application and are waiting on the final decision).

It's also possible to patent a chemical formula (like the recipe for Coca Cola®) or a unique process for doing something (like Amazon®'s one click ordering).

If you have an idea for an invention that might be patentable, the least expensive way to begin is to start an inventor's notebook. You can find information about them at www .createforcash.com. These specialized notebooks tell you exactly how to start legally protecting your ideas.

The second inexpensive step you might want to take is to file a provisional patent. You can find out more info at www. uspto.gov. They also have an inventor's assistance center to help answer your questions.

Patent agent Allen Hertz of Galahad Co. has this to say about the patent process:

Do all products need to be patented?

Not all products *can* be patented. You should try to protect your product utilizing any and all possible means, including patents, copyrights, trademarks, and even domain names. Each has its own unique benefits and limitations, and you should contact an intellectual property attorney for guidance, as each situation is unique. You need to ensure that you're not infringing on other patents.

What is a provisional patent, and should you start with that first or go straight to a regular patent?

A provisional patent is essentially a registration with the government that you have a product you are desiring to patent. This process allows you to continue development on your product while having some patent pending protection. There are some drawbacks that one needs to consider before filing a provisional patent. A provisional patent is not considered a "reduction to practice", whereas a utility patent is. This could be a factor should you be involved in an interference against another inventor's application. You could effectively gain up to one year of protection using this process. A provisional application should really be written and submitted as close to a non-provisional as possible to ensure the non-provisional requirements are met.

Should you keep an inventor's notebook, and does that give you any legal protection as the first person to come up with the idea?

Absolutely. Documentation is a key asset in the U.S. for determining rights and ownership. A proper logbook would be considered legally binding evidence.

When you do get a patent, should you license it to your own corporation or not?

Each case is unique and needs to be considered as such. If multiple inventors are involved, the patent should be assigned to a company and the inventors should draft an agreement between themselves early on.

What happens to patent rights if you file with someone else and the business relationship breaks up?

It's critical to have things in writing from day one. The more that is discussed and documented in advance, the better the relationship will be long-term.

How many people can you license your product to?

It can be an exclusive with one party or infinite numbers.

Should you give full license rights to one company or many different ones?

Each agreement is unique and needs to be considered on a case by case basis. One thing to remember, once you enter into a non-exclusive agreement, it is extremely difficult to pursue an exclusive agreement with another party.

Do you need to get license rights to sell someone else's patented products?

To protect yourself you should:

Copyrights

Copyright is a form of protection provided to the authors of "original works of authorship", including literary, dramatic, musical, artistic, and certain other intellectual works. This applies to both published and unpublished works.

A copyright gives the owner the right to control who can make copies of the work, so it discourages others from using your materials without your permission.

Ebooks are sometimes sold with a license to reproduce the ebook; this makes it more attractive to the buyer, as they are not just getting the book, but the rights to sell it to others.

Trademarks

According to the U.S. Department of Commerce, "A trademark may be a word, symbol, design, or combination word and design, a slogan, or even a distinctive sound, which identifies the goods and services of one party from another". For example, Coke® and Pepsi® are trademarks. Also, if you've ever heard the "Intel Inside" commercials, the sound of the tones at the end of it is also trademarked.

When marks are used to identify services, they are called service marks. They are usually treated the same as trademarks. An example would be Roto-Rooter.

Sometimes trademark protection can extend to include the packaging, color, or other aspects of the product. These features fall under the term "trade dress". If consumers associate that feature with a certain manufacturer rather than the product in general, it would be covered under the same protection.

An example of trade dress would be the unique shape of a Coca-Cola bottle, or the unique design of the ipod.

A trademark protects you as long as you provide the product or service. A trademark is abandoned when its use is discontinued with no intention of using it in the future.

It's also possible that a trademark could become generic over time and lose its protection. "Aspirin" was once a trademark, but became a generic term once people started using the term to refer to any similar headache remedy. The same thing happened to the term Xerox ä, once most people used it as a symbol for "copy".

Melissa Dagodag of the Law Offices of Melissa K. Dagodag specializes in trademark and copyright law. Melissa answers some of our questions about both:

What is the most important thing business owners need to know about copyrights and trademarks?

You want to be sure you are not stepping on someone else's toes by using a substantially similar (in the case of a copyright) image, literary work, photographic work, etc. or by using a confusingly similar (in the case of trademarks) brand name or logo. So, you should hire an attorney to search existing copyrights and trademarks before you actually start using them.

What is the difference between a copyright and a trademark? Do you need both?

These are frequently confused, and in fact are very different. A copyright gives the owner the right to control how a creative work is used and is made up of a number of exclusive rights, including the right to make copies, authorize others to make copies, make derivative works, and sell and market the work, and perform the work. In contrast, a trademark gives the owner the right to exclude others from using a confusingly similar trademark or brand name or logo (a distinctive sign or indicator used by an individual, business, or other entity to identify that the products or services with which the trademark appears originate from a unique source and distinguish its products or services from those of other entities.)

Do you need to protect everything with a copyright or trademark?

It's not a question of necessity. If you want to minimize your chances of being sued for trademark or copyright infringement, then it's a good idea to have an attorney run a trademark or copyright search before you begin using a trademark or publishing an image, design, or photograph, etc. that may be copyrighted. Federal registration of both copyrights and trademarks may also give the owner certain rights to statutory damages in the event of an infringement of the owner's copyright or trademark that the owner will lose if the owner does not have a federal registration.

How long is your work covered by a copyright or trademark?

The term or duration of a copyright in the U.S. is generally the life of the author plus seventy-five years if the work is created today. If it was created in the past, the rules are more complicated. You can go to www.uspto.gov to learn more. As far as trademarks are concerned, the way one gains and keeps ownership of a trademark is through actual use of the mark on goods or in connection with services. Therefore, as long as one continues to use the mark in commerce, one keeps the trademark alive. The duration of a trademark is therefore potentially unlimited.

What is the most important thing business owners need to know about copyrights and trademarks?

You want to be sure you are not stepping on someone else's toes by using a substantially similar (in the case of a copyright) image, literary work, photographic work, etc. or by using a confusingly similar (in the case of trademarks) brand name or logo. So, you should hire an attorney to search existing copyrights and trademarks before you actually start using them.

What is the difference between a copyright and a trademark? Do you need both?

These are frequently confused, and in fact are very different. A copyright gives the owner the right to control how a creative work is used and is made up of a number of exclusive rights, including the right to make copies, authorize others to make copies, make derivative works, and sell and market the work, and perform the work. In contrast, a trademark gives the owner the right to exclude others from using a confusingly similar trademark or brand name or logo (a distinctive sign or indicator used by an individual, business, or other entity to identify that the products or services with which the trademark appears originate from a unique source and distinguish its products or services from those of other entities.)

Do you need to protect everything with a copyright or trademark?

It's not a question of necessity. If you want to minimize your chances of being sued for trademark or copyright infringement, then it's a good idea to have an attorney run a trademark or copyright search before you begin using a trademark or publishing an image, design, or photograph, etc. that may be copyrighted. Federal registration of both copyrights and trademarks may also give the owner certain rights to statutory damages in the event of an infringement of the owner's copyright or trademark that the owner will lose if the owner does not have a federal registration.

How long is your work covered by a copyright or trademark?

The term or duration of a copyright in the U.S. is generally the life of the author plus seventy-five years if the work is created today. If it was created in the past, the rules are more complicated. You can go to www.uspto.gov to learn more. As far as trademarks are concerned, the way one gains and keeps ownership of a trademark is through actual use of the mark on goods or in connection with services. Therefore, as long as one continues to use the mark in commerce, one keeps the trademark alive. The duration of a trademark is therefore potentially unlimited.

Trade Secrets

Trade secrets are information that your business would want to keep secret from competitors, and whose value comes from the fact that it isn't widely known. Examples might include customer lists, or unique ways (that only your business knows about) of delivering services that enable you to outperform the competition.

Patent attorney and Founder of IPWatchdog, Inc. Gene Quinn explains why businesses should have trade secret protection:

Trade secrets are a very important part of any intellectual property portfolio. It's not much of an overstatement to say that virtually every business has trade secrets worth protection, regardless of whether the business is run as a sole proprietorship, a small business, or a Fortune 500 company. Perhaps it's better to say that every business has assets that could and should be protected as trade secrets, but the truth is that many companies, even large companies, fail to do so properly.

Trade secret protection can exist for virtually any business information. And trade secret is extremely easy to obtain.

By definition, a trade secret is any business information that is valuable because it is a secret. While most consider trade secrets to be synonymous with inventions, that is an oversimplification. It is, of course, true that trade secrets exist for most, if not all inventions, but trade secret protection can be had for such things as customer, vendor, or supplier lists. This is true because your customer lists and supplier lists are something that you benefit from keeping away from potential competitors. If a competitor could obtain your customer list and just solicit them, the competitor would have lessened or eliminated the need for advertising expenses because they are starting with a targeted list of people who are already predisposed to being interested.

Trade secrets are easy to protect because all the law requires is that you take reasonable precautions to keep the information a secret. What is reasonable will vary depending on the value of the business information, but keeping things such as customer lists in a filing cabinet in a locked office and stamping the file "Confidential" are relatively low cost efforts and should be employed. Any other efforts you take are certainly helpful, but you must do something.

So, what is the downside of trade secret protection? As with many things that are easy to acquire, they are also easy to lose. As soon as the trade secret is no longer a secret, you have lost all protection. Trade secrets are indeed fragile. So this means that while you can and should keep trade secrets, and take reasonable efforts to protect them, if other forms of intellectual property are available, you should at least consider them.

WHAT WILL YOU SELL?

Your topics may lead you to create products, services, or combinations of both. We'll talk about many different ways of creating businesses, and along the way, you should find some that fit best for your particular topics, skills, and ideas.

First, let's talk about product-based businesses. If you are skilled in making things, you might plan to make chairs and tables from PCV pipe and start an outdoor furniture making business.

If you are artistically inclined, you might purchase baskets and straw filler, and mix that with unique, artistically presented items to create attractive gifts for a gift basket business.

Or, if you have an inventive mind, you might come up with a patentable invention (like I did with swiggies).

In any case, whatever product you devise, you should be thinking ahead as to how you will sell it, and how you will sell as much as possible.

Getting customers is one of the most difficult aspects of any new business, so once you have them, you'll want to sell as much as possible to them so you aren't as dependent on finding new customers.

It's important to consider how to maximize sales to customers even in the very early planning stage of your business, because it may help you decide what is best to sell—*and* to plan what additional items might go well with your basic product.

How do you sell the maximum amount to your customers? There are two ways: sell additional items (upsales), or sell repeatedly to the same customers (consumables and continuity programs).

UPSALES

An "upsale" is an additional product or service that you can offer to someone who has just purchased your product. It should be something that makes sense for the buyer, and that adds extra profits for you, the seller.

From our earlier examples, let's say you just sold someone a pair of outdoor PVC pipe chairs and tables. One possible upsale would be to offer a third chair and table for a reduced price. Another upsale would be to offer delivery and setup for an extra charge.

Or, you could find an inexpensive source for outdoor umbrellas, and offer these (for a profit) to your furniture buyers.

For the gift basket example, you could offer to deliver the basket for an extra charge. And, if you're musically talented, you might offer a singing telegram to go with it, to make the gift even more special for the recipient (and more profitable for you).

In the case of swiggies, the wrist water bottle, I developed a sports drink mix, which served as a logical upsale to anyone who bought swiggies.

Whatever you develop, definitely include some upsales as part of your planning.

CONSUMABLES AND CONTINUITY PROGRAMS

A consumable is something a buyer will purchase and use, then need to replace. Some examples would be food and drink products, batteries, razors, office supplies, vitamins, and skincare products.

I created a new all natural, sugar-free drink mix so I would have something to sell with the swiggies wrist water bottles for kids. I packaged them in stick form and called them swiggie stix. After hearing parents complain about electrolyte drinks that are artificial and loaded with sugar, I thought this would be a great add-on to the line. Parents liked them because they were all natural and sugar-free and kids liked them because they tasted just like sugar.

I tested it with some very hard-core athletes and found out that they were also looking for a product like this. Now I have it packaged in swiggie stix for kids and under the Hydro-Sport brand name for athletes. Same package, different markets. But in any case, it's a consumable my customers will buy again and again.

The other way to get repeat purchases is a continuity program. A continuity program involves shipping a product out to a customer that they have asked for on a continuous basis. Most people will stay on the program for an average of 4–6 months. Find a product your customers can't live without, and then keep selling it to them on a regular basis. As long as it lives up to their expectations, they will probably keep buying it.

If you want to be involved with consumables, you might want to check out some of the multilevel marketing companies that sell vitamins, household goods, and so on. It's an easy way to get into the business of selling something people need repeatedly. But be careful, since there are many MLM companies that vanish as quickly as they appear.

If you are even more entrepreneurial, you could do a Goggle search for "private label" plus whatever type of consumable you would like to market, i.e., private label vitamins. You can find plenty of companies who will manufacture for you with your label and company name on the product, and you just take care of the marketing.

Even if you have regular customers in a continuity program, you still need to make sure you communicate with them on a consistent basis. Let them know about any improvements and make sure they are still happy with your service. Find a great consumable or continuity program for your product line, and you'll have customers for life.

UNIQUE BUSINESS CONCEPTS

It's okay to start small with your Money Garden businesses, but some of you have big ideas. If you come up with a unique business concept, you may find yourself with the kind of idea that attracts investors like a magnet and enables you to make a huge start.

Just what do I mean by "unique business concept"? A unique business concept is basically one that hasn't been done before. The best way I can explain unique business concepts is by example. Here are some examples of cutting edge, innovative business concepts:

Ebay

EBay was originally called AuctionWeb. It's founder, Pierre Omidyar, was doing an experiment on how equal access to information and opportunities would effect the efficiency of marketplaces. He placed a broken laser printer on the auction site for $14.83, which sold to the highest bidder. He contacted the bidder to make sure he knew the laser pointer was broken. He bought it anyway. Since then the company was built on the core values and a belief that people are basically good, everyone has something to contribute, and an open environment brings out the best in people. EBay is an innovative business concept that combined an auction with an online site.

FedEx

Fed Ex was originally built on the concept of delivering spare parts through an integrated system and nationwide clearinghouse. Document delivery wasn't permitted until 1978 because the Postal Service had a monopoly on delivering mail. As long as Fed Ex delivered something overnight and charged twice as much as the First Class postage, then it was exempt from the monopoly. Company-owned planes would free the service from commercial airline schedules and shipping regulations, while a single hub would keep control over the packages that "Absolutely, positively had to be there overnight."

Netflix

Reed Hastings had the idea for Netflix after being forced to pay $40 in fines for an overdue videotape rental. DVDs had just been introduced and few people owned a DVD player. But Hastings saw the future potential and took the plunge by launching Netflix, a mail order DVD rental service. A subscription service was offered that charged monthly and had no late fees.

In and Out Burger

In 1948 Harry Snyder came up with the idea of having a drive-thru hamburger stand where customers could order through a two-way speaker box. This business concept was quite unique and quickly caught on as a replacement for the carhops who used to service customers that wanted to order from their car. Today the concept of the drive-thru has branched out into banking, drugstores, coffee shops, and even drive-thru weddings in Vegas.

If you come up with a unique business concept, it's more important then ever to put together a business plan, as this will be the tool you use to attract capital from investors. Here's an example of a unique business concept called "Sample Rewards" put together by a pair of very prolific businesspeople:

Billy and Julie Carmen of Wizard Industries have a very unique business model which is also covered by a methodology patent. Here is what makes their business different:

Wizard Distribution started with one product, which was invented by Billy, and has grown into over 60 new products, along with a distribution channel with hundreds of other brands.

Billy and Julie used their knowledge and experience gained in engineering, designing and building a database-driven e-commerce and social networking technology to create a powerful news development and distribution entity, a product manufacturing and distribution company, and a marketing, e-commerce and product launch system called Small Brand Nation/Product News Channel.

This is a system consisting of dozens of additional markets and topic specific websites, along with a magazine called Product News Journal that allows enthusiastic consumers to learn about new products and refer Wizard Distribution products to retailers through the SampleRewards.com website. So, if a consumer finds a product they like, they refer the product to their local retailers. If the product line is picked up by the retailer, the consumer gets the product for free. It's a win-win for everyone involved.

This two-pronged approach, along with the exposure built through news and social media has proven to be a very powerful marketing, exposure, and sales tool for Wizard Industries and the products distributed through the system.

SampleRewards.com was able to secure a methodology and technology patent because of its unique business method that combines the most advanced computer and Internet technologies to allow new products to rapidly enter the national market through what has been called "viral marketing" or direct public support. It's basically "one-stop shopping" for new products going to market.

The only sales force SampleRewards.com has is the millions of people who alert retailers to new Wizard products.

SELLING INFORMATION

Everybody is an expert at something. Whoever you are, you have a wealth of knowledge that someone will pay to learn. First you need to find a market for your knowledge. Who needs to learn what you have to teach? Even better if what you have is a niche market. Do you know how to knit dog clothes? Keep bugs out of your flower garden? Feed a family in the cheapest and best way possible? Be a big fish in a small pond and be unique.

Once you know your customer, take them on a step-by-step journey of what *you've* accomplished and what *they* can accomplish if they follow your advice. Narrow your topic down to find a niche market. A general book about animals might be hard to sell, but a book about how to raise ferrets will find buyers. And they'll be really excited to read your book.

If you're not a good writer, find someone who is. Pay a ghostwriter or co-write with someone else in the field. Your books or tapes should be done in a conversational tone with a sense of humor, some relatable stories, and some case studies.

Sell information on one of your hobbies. Why not? You enjoy doing it anyway. Writing about something you enjoy makes it that much easier and much more fun.

Find a need in the market by watching the news and tuning in to what's happening in the world. What kinds of trends are out there? Where are they headed? What are people frustrated about and what do they need? Help them fill that need.

Quality books will always sell. Create the best products possible. Create low, medium, and higher priced products. Give customers a choice. Encourage feedback from your customers. Get them to ask you questions. And add perceived value by including a money back guarantee and having customer testimonials.

If you're selling an ebook, you can offer to give potential buyers a free download of part one to interest them in the rest. Have a good presentation with a cleverly designed cover, and marketing materials that look professional so they'll be interested in owning the whole package.

I can't tell you how many times people would call and ask if I had anything else to sell. If they have a good experience with you once, they'll want to keep buying from you. Customers will buy from you when they trust you. So, always be creating new products so you'll have more to sell.

Information products include:

- Ebooks and printed books
- Reports

- Audio files on tape or CD
- DVDs
- DVD/workbook
- Private website membership with access to information

Another way to sell information is to compile a directory. You do all the work to put together specialized information to sell to a targeted market. I remember being on a film set and seeing a girl who was selling a directory of casting opportunities for people who wanted to be extras. She was working on the set, getting paid, and selling her directory to the other people who were working as extras and really wanted the information. She was a good example of someone who understands the Money Garden concept by generating income from two sources at the same time.

NON-PROFIT ORGANIZATIONS

According to Wikipedia, "a non-profit organization is a legally constituted organization whose objective is to support or engage in activities of public or private interest without any external commercial or monetary profit." Non-profit organizations use their profits to advance their programs, while for-profits give the profits to the stockholders.

If you have a business idea that will benefit the community or a large group of people, then a non-profit is the way to go. Do good for the world and get paid for it. Your salary and benefits are set by the Board of Directors. But you're entitled to a competitive salary that complies with IRS guidelines.

You should pick a charity that you will be passionate about. What could be better than having an income stream that also helps other people and feeds on your own enthusiasm?

According to the Society for Non-Profit Organizations, here are the basic things you need to do to start a non-profit:

1. Define your organization's purpose and form, and write a mission statement. Your mission statement should explain why people would want to invest in your organization.
2. Form a Board of Directors.
3. File articles of incorporation. If you don't incorporate, board members and other individuals in your organization may be held personally liable in case of a lawsuit. Articles of incorporation should be filed with your Secretary of State or other department that has authority for this filing in your state.
4. Write your organization's bylaws or the rules you will adhere to.
5. Apply for non-profit status from the IRS. (ask your local IRS office for publication 557 and IRS form 1023)
6. After you have received your letter of determination from the IRS, apply to your State Department of Revenue and your state department in charge of regulations, often called the Department of Regulation and Licensing.
7. Register your organization with the state. Contact the Secretary of State (corporate division) and Attorney General (charities division).
8. Apply for a solicitation license from your city. Check to see if your city requires you to have such a license before you can solicit funds.

9. Apply for a sales tax exemption from your state.
10. Apply for a non-profit bulk mail permit from your post office.
11. Obtain liability insurance, including Directors and Officers insurance. This is necessary to protect your board member's assets.

You can check out books at Nolo.com for a step-by-step guide that includes all the forms needed to start a non-profit.

And if you have a knack for fundraising, the non-profit is a good place for you. Again, your selling skills and your networking and social skills will be put to use.

People give money to non-profits because they want to feel generous and compassionate. And they also want to change the world. You should be working your non-profit because it's something that you're passionate about and therefore you'll feel good about raising money for it. You should believe in it.

Think of your non-profit just like you would the other businesses in your Money Garden. Market them in some of the same ways with direct mail, events, newsletters, and Internet marketing. Non-profits tend to get publicity because of the nature of what they do.

Also, Google Grants gives free search advertising to non-profits who have 501 (c) (3) status, a website, and are not affiliated with political or religious groups. They pick new grantees every quarter.

Another good reason to start a non-profit is the huge amount of grant money available to them. Grants are competitive, but even small non-profits with grant writers can secure them. And unlike loans that a business might take out, grants never have to be repaid. You can find grant writers online, and if one believes in your case, they might even volunteer to help you.

Pamela Hawley of Universal Giving goes into more detail:

What are the right and wrong reasons to start a non-profit?

Starting a non-profit must come from the head and the heart. It's a true balance. Most people think you need to have strong passion and loyalty to a cause, and you do. But one must also have a strong desire for effective business planning and operations in order to ensure you deliver your product, in this case, service to the community, effectively. At the same time, you can't be 'all business', but we are compassionately serving others in very dire circumstances. In the world of Universal Giving we are helping people who live on $800 annually, which is 70% of the world.

This balanced viewpoint of head and heart is often more identified long the lines of social entrepreneurship. It's often also tied into revenue.

The wrong reason to start a non-profit is because you think it's a 'cush' job or comes with less demands. Your responsibility increases. Fundraising is tough. And, if you fail to deliver, you are dealing with people's lives and the fact that they might not receive truly dire services. Your job can become one of helping others through life and death. It's not just that your product line failed; here a lifeline could have failed.

How do you determine your salary?

The board determines the CEO's salary. We take into account whether the position is full-time or part-time, qualifications (past entrepreneurial experience), results, fundraising success, and business qualifications. We also look at comparative compensation across similar size non-profits, in similar locales with cost of living.

***Are there other ways to raise money for your non-profit besides
grant writing and fundraising?***

Absolutely. In fact, I believe non-profits should be able to monetize some
part of their service in order to demonstrate market interest and increase and
diversify their funding. For example, Universal Giving allows people to give
and volunteer with the top-performing projects around the world. We vet
all organizations and projects with a 10-stage Quality Model. 100% of your
donation goes to the non-profit. So this service is free to the public because we
want people to give with trust and transparency, and to get as much funds to
deserving people as possible.

    So, how do we do this? We also have a customized service, Universal Giving
Corporate, which helps companies launch their CSR programs. We help them
lead and manage their international giving and volunteer programs. We set up
programs in the cities where their employees live and work, vet non-profits,
market out to their employees to increase giving and volunteer results. All of
this helps companies operate on the global level, increase their brand, and
increase employee and client loyalty. Universal Giving is paid to perform these
services, which also meet our mission.

    Therefore, I highly recommend non-profits provide both services, which
supports their mission and their long-term financial viability.

***Do you need to have an attorney set up your non-profit
or can you do it yourself?***

You can set up the 501 (c) (3) structure yourself. You can find a book that will
help you walk through the process. It's not difficult, but it does take some time.
I did do it myself for Universal Giving, however you can pay an attorney to do
it for about $3,000–$5,000. Some attorneys may do it pro bono. As a non-profit
professional, you should consider pro bono services as a constant part of your
resources.

    Pamela Hawley is CEO of UniversalGiving.org, a social entrepreneurship
non-profit organization whose vision is to "create a world where giving and
volunteering is a natural part of every day life."

EVENTS

I can't count the number of trade shows I've done and one thing is clear. No matter how bad the show was for me or anyone else who paid to be there, the one person that always made money was the company that put on the show. Think about it. They made money from selling the booth space. Who's to say you couldn't do the same thing?

> **Tip**
>
> Use your imagination and come up with the most unique event you can think of:
>
> ■ Trade show
> ■ Music event
> ■ Golf tournament
> ■ Kid's event
> ■ Food show

Like I mentioned in the beginning, you should create your own products and services *and* sell other people's. This includes events. Be creative and create your own events, and you can also create events for others and get paid for it. What kind of event hasn't been done before?

Tyler Cassidy, a cemetery entrepreneur, bought the Hollywood Forever Cemetery, where such movie legends as Rudolph Valentino and Jayne Mansfield are buried. Then he got the great idea of combining movies and mausoleums and began showing movies on the mausoleum wall. He was then approached by the founder of Cinespia, a film society dedicated to showing classic films. The film society has a new home and the event has grown. They now show films there throughout the summer. Who can *you* partner with to come up with a unique event?

The haunted house industry even has its own association (HHA) and their own magazine, Haunt World Magazine. Can you come up with a more unique haunted house? What about a unique Easter Egg hunt? Or Christmas event?

If you've ever been to a Renaissance Faire, you know how unique and profitable it can be. There are hundreds of Renaissance Faires that go on every year.

Each night of the summer in Laguna Beach, California, the Festival of the Arts presents its most famous attraction, The Pageant of the Masters. The highly successful pageant is ninety minutes of "living pictures" or art re-creations of classical and contemporary works using live people to pose exactly like their counterparts in the original works. The living art pieces are set to an original music score with professional lighting.

This unique festival has been running as a successful non-profit for years and was started during The Great Depression to help draw visitors to the Laguna Beach art community. That proves that you can start a business any time, especially during hard, economic times when you have to be more creative.

And, who could forget P.T. Barnum's "Greatest Show on Earth"? LIFE magazine called him "the patron saint of promoters" and one of the most important people of the millennium. One of his first sideshows featured a woman who claimed to be 161 years old. Then he purchased a museum in New York City that exhibited 500,000 curiosities from around the world. He kept people moving at a quick pace and placed a sign at the end that said "This way to the egress". People were curious to see what an egress looked like, but found themselves outside, as "egress" turned out to be the exit. And they had to pay another quarter if they wanted to see the show again. For anyone who thinks they're too old to start a business, Barnum was sixty years old when he took his traveling circus on the road. The rest is history.

One of the wackiest events I've seen is the Hash Harriers, which evolved from the original hunting sport of Hares and Hounds. It's a worldwide event with thousands of loyal fans in over 180 countries. They are billed as "A drinking club with a running problem". Started in 1938 by a Brit named Albert Stephen Ignatius Gispert, the event has grown to over 1800 hashes in almost every major city in the world. The modern version is more of a non-competitive social event where you join the pack of hounds (runners) and follow a trail set by the hares (other runners) and meet up for a social activity known as the On-On where drinks and snacks are served. There are hashes for kids, families, and adults' only pub-crawls. Some are special events where everyone dresses in costume. But the one thing you must bring is your sense of humor.

Start a small, intimate event or plan something as elaborate as Barnum. It could be an event that runs every week or a big yearly bash. It could be a traveling event or one that stays in one place.

Here are some more ideas to get you thinking. How can you make them more unique?

- Auction
- Bake sale
- Block party
- Beach party

- Business luncheon
- Car wash
- Cook-off contest
- Fashion show
- Festival
- Garage sale
- Marathon
- Movie night
- Talent show
- Tournament
- Treasure hunt
- Wedding

Tip

Here are some ideas to generate more profit at an event:

1 Sell raffle tickets (but check local regulations first)
2 Corporate sponsorships
3 Silent auctions
4 Coupon books given to guests, but paid for by advertisers
5 Get products donated
6 Donate some of your own products for added exposure

Create an event around a sporting event. For example, marathons are big business. What other sporting events can you think of? What kind of events do you enjoy yourself? Someone came up with the hot dog eating contest and the tractor pull. Look how big the NASCAR events became.

What kind of fun event can you come up with? The whole point of this book is to be creative, have fun, and make money at the same time.

Events generate a lot of publicity. Make yours unique and grab some headlines.

SOCIAL NETWORKS

A social network is a group of people drawn together by work, family, or hobby. Professor J.A. Barnes first coined the phrase and defined a social network as a group of about 100 to 150 people.

Social networking sites become a virtual community for people who are interested in a common subject. Members create their own profile and communicate with each other through email, IM, or meeting in person.

This is based on the six degrees of separation concept that each person is only six steps away from every other person in the world. Social networking sites allow you to connect with people that you normally wouldn't meet for friendship, jobs, marriage, etc.

When you think of social networking, sites like My Space, Facebook, and Twitter come to mind. These are heavily funded by venture capitalists. But an email network is something that you can start from scratch and build up. An email network consists of regular emails sent to a mailing list, and based around some common interest such as job listings, discounts and bargains, clean jokes, and so on. It's easy to start and you can build one by posting in relevant online forums, and by encouraging happy users to spread the word to their contacts. Blogs, with their ability to allow users to comment, participate, and contribute can also be considered a type of social network. (more on blogs later)

Traxee.com is a social networking community where women runners can come together, inspire and support each other in all stages of the sport, from running for fitness, to training, to competition. Traxee's distinctly female perspective on the athletic lifestyle reflects the essential balance between strength of body to strength of spirit. Through a fun, supportive environment of like-minded women, comprehensive content, expert advice, the latest product information, and reviews and innovative, interactive tools, Traxee community members can set, track, achieve and celebrate their goals "on the track" and in life.

Co-founder, Beth Moore, explains how Traxee got its start:

Opportunity sometimes meets us in the most unusual places. For me, opportunity came over sizzling shrimp in a popular L.A. restaurant.

Having spent years working as a corporate marketing executive, I was searching for a way to turn my personal passion for distance running into something more than just a hobby. My best friend and business partner, Julie Running (yes, that really is her last name), just happened to be married to one of the founders of Tuesday Creative—a successful interactive agency here in L.A. that was interested in developing a social networking project from the ground up. Julie and I pitched the concept for Traxee to the principals of Tuesday Creative over dinner. They loved the idea, and we were off, and well, running.

I believe that the greatest gift in life is to work at something about which you are truly passionate. I started running 18 years ago in a desperate search for improvements in my health. A reformed 2-pack a day sedentary smoker, I am well aware of the physical, mental, and emotional benefits of running. The sport literally saved my life and the Traxee project was the opportunity I had been waiting for to share my passion.

Of course, having passion and vision does not a viable business make. Women's running is one of the fastest-growing segments in non-professional sports, and there is a lot of competition from sports magazine publishers, news aggregators, product manufacturing giants, and other social networking start-ups in this segment. The challenge is to attract significant numbers of members that will actively participate in online conversation. Seems straightforward enough, right?

As I have learned over the past year, success in the social networking space is a combination of science and art. The quickest way to build an online community is to build awareness through best SEM (search engine marketing) practices (the "science"), and by relentlessly creating content that is interesting and valuable to your audience (the "art"). It's incredibly time-consuming, which is why it's so helpful to be passionate about what you're doing.

I am constantly torn about the types of content we should be providing at Traxee. Our data tells me that pieces about weight loss and cellulite draws hundreds more readers than other types of posts.

The temptation is always to simply create more of that type of content. Yet my vision for Traxee is a little different. Women are constantly bombarded with information about beauty and weight loss. I want to talk about what it feels like to cross the finish line after running 26.2 miles!

Of course, the principal way money is made through social networking is with advertising, affiliate partnerships, and ultimately the sale of the business. This spring Traxee will begin a formal advertising program as a publisher. To get our ad rates up, to build value and create partnerships with others, we need to generate more traffic and participation on the site. To do that we have to create high-demand content.

There is a huge opportunity right now for women in social networking and the Web 2.0 space in general. We humans are natural communicators and we love sharing what we know with others. Google just about any topic on the planet and you'll find tons of women bloggers, artists, and businesswomen from all over the world actively and openly exchanging ideas.

For product marketers, the online social space can provide valuable feedback for continuous improvement. Small business owners and service providers can use social networks to build solid credentials and establish levels of expertise for their businesses. Best of all you don't have to have a fancy agency or years of technology experience to take advantage of these tools . . . just a few seconds to set up an account on Blogger. Then just apply your passion!

FRANCHISING

Franchising is a topic of interest for your Money Garden in two different ways. First, you might be interested in a low-cost franchise as one of your first businesses. They are available in all different price ranges and areas of interest.

Or, much more profitable in the long run is for you to create a business which can later be franchised (where you are the franchisor).

If you create a business with a great name, and strong logos and trademarks, plus a profitable operation that can be duplicated and taught to others, then you have a business that is a candidate for franchising. Since I want to encourage you to dream big, let's talk a little more in detail about franchising.

According to Wikipedia "franchising refers to the methods of practicing and using another person's philosophy of business. The franchisor grants the independent operator the right to distribute its products, techniques and trademarks for a percentage of gross monthly sales and a royalty fee. Various tangibles and intangibles such as advertising, training or other support services are commonly made available by the franchisor".

The principles of franchising date back to the mid 1800's. Royalties or fees were collected on a product basis instead of gross sales of the business operations. At the beginning of the 1900s General Motors started franchising their dealerships. By the 1930s the gasoline and soft drink industries had entered the industry.

Franchising became more popular with the increase in fast food restaurants and motel chains. These succeeded because people like to frequent businesses and buy products they are familiar with and which are consistent.

In the 1970s several states regulated franchising, and by 1979 the Federal Trade Commission did also. Today, the Federal Trade Commission defines a franchise as a business relationship where the owner uses a common name, receives training from the parent company, and pays a fee to the parent company.

Franchises are usually either "product and trade name" franchises, where the franchisor is the manufacturer for a franchisee wholesaler, or "business format" franchises, which doesn't involve a manufactured product.

Some examples of well-known franchises include:

- McDonald's
- Marriott
- Buick
- A & W Root Beer
- Harley-Davidson
- Domino's Pizza
- Jenny Craig
- Re-Max
- Blockbuster Video
- 7-Eleven
- Coldwell-Banker
- H & R Block
- Burger King
- Pearle Vision

Franchising actually picks up when good jobs are lost in a bad economy because franchisees can create their own jobs. They usually have a better success rate than independent businesses because they are a carbon copy of a business that has already proven itself to be successful.

Since this is a book about owning your own business, you may get to a point where you will want to franchise your own business. Not all businesses are suitable for franchising and not everyone is suitable for being a franchisor. But if you want to take that path, you'll need to educate yourself on running a very different type of business entity.

Lori Lofstrom of Holmes & Lofstrom, LLP reveals the 7 qualities of successful franchisors:

1. Keep it simple.

Complicated concepts including multi-unit franchising, area development programs, or those dramatically outside the norm can come later. Avoid significant revisions to your documents and making "special deals" that are difficult to track and compromise uniformity.

2. Find a mentor.

Try to meet with "seasoned" franchisors willing to share. This can help you avoid costly mistakes and learn proven methods to accomplish your goals successfully. Join trade organizations like the International Franchising Association.

3. Compliance program set-up.

Work with a consultant or counsel to draft a compliance checklist for you. This will help ensure that you are following the franchise sales rules and maintaining good recordkeeping.

4. **Sales process checklist.**

   Successful franchisors have a predetermined, step-by-step process through which they carefully and methodically lead each of their prospective franchisees. If a franchisee can not follow a sales process, they will probably not be able to follow your system either.

5. **Controlled growth.**

   Don't let your prospects control your growth. Set a growth plan of those states that you will expand to and stick with it. Establish a response system for prospects in states where you are not yet legal to offer or sell.

6. **Franchise communication.**

   Facilitate periodic communication with your fanchisees to get their input and feedback. Set up a Franchise Advisory Counsel once you have some interested franchisees that are not in start-up mode.

7. **Enforce your agreements.**

   When a franchisee is not following the system, it's your responsibility to the system and the other franchisees to notify and mandate that the franchisee comply. Follow the steps in the franchise agreement, but be firm so that you send a message to all.

MIDDLEMAN

If you're a go-getter and can drum up business, but can't or don't actually want to do the work involved, then be a middleman (or woman). If you have extensive connections and are a good networker, this is probably a great business for you. It's basically just introducing the buyer to the seller. You don't get involved in the sales transaction. An average finder's fee is around five per cent, but could be higher or lower depending on the item or service.

One of my businesses is a PR firm. In getting customers of my own, sometimes I would get a customer whose business I felt could be better serviced by someone else. I didn't want to lose the customer, so I had a list of really good publicists, and someone on the list always made a perfect match for them. The publicist was happy to pay me a percentage and get a customer's business that they specialized in.

If you want to use middlemen to work for you, give them enough of an incentive to want to sell for you. This is also how the affiliate programs work.

You can also be a middleman for investors or start-ups. Or anyone looking for money. It's also called a finder's fee.

Filmmakers would be glad to pay a finder's fee to get their movies produced. Someone who sells close-outs is a middleman to retailers. People will pay finder's fees for locating collectibles, locations for vending machines, equipment leasing, and for a suitable lender for a loan.

Finding rare coins and rare books is another big area. So is finding historical items for large corporations. And finding new clients for doctors, dentists and lawyers. You can also help people find roomates.

Whatever you find, you need to document the money you spend in your efforts to get your finder's fee. And you need to have a solid contract with the person paying you.

You can sometimes find opportunities in the newspaper. But one of the best ways is to network. I always ask my friends what projects they have going on, and quite often they will be willing to pay a commission to find something quickly.

The best part about being a finder is that you don't need ANY money to start, or very little money if you want to advertise your services.

SERVICES

I'll go back to what I said about doing what you're good at. Since one of your first businesses will probably be a service business, it will also probably be something that you have done as an employee. And, you will probably be doing all of the work in the beginning.

My first two businesses, which I still have, are a PR business and a script reading business. I started the PR business because I had paid thousands of dollars to a big, fancy PR firm, and all I got was a small mention in one magazine. I had to learn how to do it myself, and eventually ended up working for a large corporation doing PR. I liked the idea of having my own clients and only working for people and projects I was passionate about. That led to my own PR firm, Abbott & Klein.

Once you get your service business off the ground and you have more work than you can handle, it's time to start hiring. The script reading service started when I was in a friend's office and noticed piles and piles of scripts on the floor. I went in a couple of weeks later and they were even higher. I asked who read them all and that's when I got my first job reading scripts. I got paid fifty dollars a script to learn on the job (the best way to learn).

After getting hired freelance to do this for other companies, I had more work than I could handle. Soon I was reading at home, at coffee shops, at stoplights, in the bathtub. I couldn't keep up with them, but didn't want to lose the clients, which took me months to find. So I started contracting them out to people who I knew could read the scripts and write great summaries, with me taking a commission as a middleman!

With any service business, your goal should always be to grow the business and train others to be the "workers" so that you can focus on your role as the business "owner".

CONSULTING

Since you're already an expert in your business, why not teach others how to do it and get paid? Why not help clients solve problems and challenge them to come up with new ideas for their business?

Consultants provide advice to companies who are in trouble. You can come in and help them do something faster, better, and cheaper.

You need to have good analytical and people skills. You'll need to be a good communicator and a good listener. You should also be creative enough to come up with your own solutions to their problems. They should be solutions that nobody else has thought of; otherwise they wouldn't need you.

WEBSITES

A website can be a business in itself, or an adjunct to one of your existing businesses. But in any case, having a website

Tech consultant Ann Lasater lists these practical ideas for getting started as a consultant from her book *Wisdom at Work: How to Survive and Thrive Through Consulting*:

1. Determine what you're good at, and if there is a market for your skills. Find a need that matches your skills and fill that need. Do some market research to ensure there are clients who need what you have to offer. Be sure you have up-to-date skills for the current market, especially if you want to work in the computer field. The more versatile your computer skills, the better it is for the consulting business, but it also pays to have some other areas where you're the expert.

2. A good way to enter the consulting field is through contracting through companies at an agency; however, use these contracts to learn as much as possible. If independent consulting is your ultimate goal, keep your goal in mind and set timetables for when you want to finish your goal.

3. Prepare a mission statement and goals you want to achieve in your business.

4. Prepare a good business plan. There are many sources for learning how to write a business plan, including software that leads you through the process.

5. Obtain business counseling through a small business center or the SBA. The SBA offers free counseling through its Service Corps of Retired Executives program.

6. Learn as much as possible about business marketing, as well as constantly keeping your skills updated, through classes, reading, and practicing. If you want to be competitive in the consulting market, you need to stay in a learning mode all the time.

7. Hire a good CPA to help you with tax advice.

8. Set up a home office because you may be able to find telecommuting jobs, as more companies are realizing the benefits of telecommuting employees. It saves them money because they don't have to provide office space or equipment; and studies show that telecommuters are about 20% more productive than they are in an office.

9. Start building a business network. There are numerous network groups. Join the ones that you have a strong interest in and become active in them. These could be social or business groups. Go to these with the right attitude—an open mind, honesty, a sincere desire to be helpful to others, and a genuine interest in others. A lot of consulting work comes through word of mouth.

should be a given. I do know very successful entrepreneurs who don't even have a website, but my thinking is "Why not?" Websites are your international storefront, the central place to send your customers, and the hub of all your business transactions.

I could have placed this in the chapter on "getting the message out", but having a website can also be considered intellectual property. Many people build up a website and sell it later on when it becomes popular.

Since you're competing against millions of other sites, try to sell something unique that you can't find anywhere else. Part of the purpose of this book is to get you to think differently. If your product or service isn't that unique, at least offer a unique advantage.

Sell what people want to buy, not what you want to sell them. Think about it from their point of view. What will the product or service do for them?

Tips on creating websites that work:

- You should be able to tell what the website is about and what it's selling within about five seconds.
- Your website should identify and solidify your brand name and image. This is what customers will use to quickly decide whether they want to do business with you or not.
- Make sure your corporate logo is at the top of every page of your website and your copyright on each page at the bottom.
- Make customers feel comfortable doing business with

you. Let them know their information is secure and private.

■ In the future, you might also want to think about joining an organization such as TRUSTe or the BBBOnline program to build trust with your customers and make them feel better about giving out their personal information.

■ You might want to add an "About Us" page. It makes you look more friendly and approachable, and lets customers know about your company or products and services.

■ After you've considered the best name for your business and brainstormed your best branding direction, register it. GoDaddy is a great place to start. They make it simple, inexpensive, and their customer service is the best. You can call them any time for advice, twenty-four hours a day, and they'll talk you through it.

■ Make sure you have a good, clean, professional looking site that is easy to navigate through, and easy to buy through. Avoid too much flash, and avoid scrolling marquee text if you can. It's hard to read and not compatible with all browsers.

■ Your site design should be consistent. That includes colors and fonts. Pick your colors carefully as they'll have a specific psychological effect on your customers. Look through websites and see what colors they use and what they're selling. It may be subconscious, but it's still an important part of your overall site.

■ Avoid having too many large graphics. It takes too long

to load, and these days people have very short attention spans. Give them their information as quickly and easily as possible.

- Have a navigation bar at the top of every page. A search engine might not index the home page, so you want visitors to search through your whole site easily.
- Avoid excessive advertising and clutter. You want your website message to be clear and to the point.
- Eliminate autoplay and make background sounds optional.
- Avoid large blocks of text. Most people will scan it anyway, so make it easy to read with bullet points and headers.
- Give your customers something new and exciting to see at your site. Give them free stuff and free articles that relate to what you're selling.
- Give them a money back guarantee. Your sales will increase if they have a win-win situation.
- Make sure they can contact you several ways, and make sure you respond quickly to their inquiries.
- Make it easy for your customers to buy when they're ready to buy. It's surprising how many companies make the process of buying difficult. (I even admit I've made this mistake before without knowing it.)
- Have a "place order" button at the bottom of every page. You might also want to let them know when to expect delivery.
- You don't necessarily have to have a call center, but you should at least provide them with a phone number for

customer service. I've also found that a lot of people still want to talk to a live person before they place an order. Make sure they can. And if it goes to voicemail, make sure you get back to them as soon as possible.

- Check to make sure your orders are going through. Place a test order yourself. I had to do this myself to make sure the order system was working. Turns out it wasn't. But I never would have figured it out if I hadn't tested it myself.

- Get a shopping cart that uses secure encryption of personal data. Most shoppers won't enter their credit card into a non-secure site.

- Check your site occasionally for dead links and download time. In fact, you should check it out completely from time to time and give it a tune-up.

- If you have an item that is out of stock, let the customer know it before they waste their time going through the whole shopping cart.

- Make sure every page in your site has a link back to the home page in case a URL is forwarded. You don't want anyone to get a dead-end.

- Get an editor to proofread your site before launching it.

- Once you're up and running, start an area for testimonials and press coverage.

Your website will be a work in progress. Just get it started and add to it later. You should be constantly testing what works and what doesn't work. Get feedback from your friends, customers, and mentors.

If you have specialized knowledge about a certain industry you might want to start a B2B, or Business to Business website. Save a company time and money, plus give them the customer service they ask for and you could do well in a B2B business. You'll be selling to other businesses, but not to the end user.

Two of the best ways to promote your site are through search engines and links from other sites. Submit your own site or hire someone to do it for you. Submission services allow you to submit to hundreds of search sites at a time.

Using keywords effectively:

Keywords are what search engines (like Google) use to rank your website. Here are some tips to improve your search engine ranking. If these are too technical, go over them with your favorite computer person!

- Create a list of keywords. Search engines use keywords to determine your website's ranking. Create as many keywords as you can. These can be nouns, verbs, adjectives, and combinations of all of these, but whichever they are they should describe terms that you would logically search for to find your specific website.
- Use multiple keywords together in a search phrase to cut down on your competition. For example, instead of "water bottles" I would put "unique water bottles".
- Put your keywords in order with the most important ones first. The number of keywords that can be submitted depends on the directory you're submitting to.
- Go to Google Ad Words and click on the keyword tool.

Put in some of your keywords to test them out and see what comes up. See how much competition you have with your competitors and what people tend to click on. The broader the keyword, the more advertising is already being done.

- Don't try to dupe the search engines by repeating words over and over hidden in your HTML and Meta tags (called keyword stuffing) or hiding keywords in your document in a small font.

- All of your keywords should be on your page and related to your page.

- Don't repeat keywords in your document by making the text the same color as the background color. Search engines are wise to this old trick.

- Don't try to trick them by making frequent title changes to look like your site is a new site. If you changed your site, resubmit it to the search engines. Make sure the search engines have your most recent website in its cache.

Submitting to directories and search engines:

Directory submission is one of the best ways to get traffic to your site. Submit to as many search engines and directories as possible. You can also submit each page because they're all different. They should each have a different title, description, and keywords. This increases your chances of being found by people searching for different keywords, etc.

If the search engine allows doorway pages, then submit those. Doorway pages are also called gateway pages and are pages that lead to your site, but aren't really considered part of your site. Don't include gateway pages on your sitemap, and don't allow pages within your site to link to them. By giving gateway pages different names you can easily see which one of them is bringing in the most traffic.

Register your site individually to the directories and search engines instead of through multiple submission sites. Keep records of your submissions and note the date, description and keywords used, page URL, and any other relevant information. Find the best category for your site, and if there are multiple categories where your site fits, submit separately for all that are suitable. Describe your site accurately since a real editor may be reviewing it.

More tips to improve your website:

- Once you have your site up and you've started marketing it, sign up for Google Alerts. It will monitor where your site is mentioned through Google and is good for staying current on your particular industry, and for monitoring the competition. It's also a good way to check for infringers if you have any intellectual property, and to find out if your website or products are being picked up by the media or other websites.
- Set up an autoresponder to answer your incoming email requests. Besides the fact that they respond to emails right away, you can get one that will grab the email address and put it in a text file.
- Win some awards. Nominate your site for an appropriate award in your industry. You can also drive traffic by nominating other sites.

- Add a link to your site that says "Bookmark" or "Add to your favorites" or "Recommend this site to a friend".
- If you have a content site, you can submit it to an announcement service. They don't review or recommend sites, they just announce them.
- Give your customers a reason to come back to your site by giving them something of value.
- Add a tip of the day that relates to your business to get people to come back to your site. Ask your visitors if they want to receive it via email. This will help you build an email list and keep visitors connected to your site.
- Start a frequent buyer program for your product or website. This is especially good if you are selling a consumable product. Set up a simple point system so your customers can win prizes as they purchase more.
- Thank your customers for coming back to your website. Send them personalized thank you's.

PROCESSING YOUR WEB ORDERS:

When I first started out I used PayPal to process credit cards. It's simple and inexpensive to use. It's free to set up, you don't have to buy any equipment, and you can start accepting payments right away.

You can easily send bills to your customers and even set up recurring monthly bill payments. PayPal is available in 190 countries, although there's an extra step involved in processing international orders because of different shipping charges. And you can upgrade your account as your business grows.

Also, in the beginning I shipped everything out myself. It's quite time consuming, but I didn't have the money to have them shipped from a fulfillment house. I had boxes in my apartment stacked to the ceiling. I didn't see the bottom of my shower in one bathroom for years.

A typical day consisted of boxing up orders, inputting information into QuickBooks, driving to the post office, driving to UPS, driving back home and doing it all over again. Then I spent the rest of the time answering emails and getting a little marketing done. I eventually moved the inventory into a warehouse and made trips every week to get more, and shipped everything from the post office.

If you're just starting out, I would still suggest doing your own shipping until you get your business to the point where it just doesn't make sense anymore. At some point your time will become more valuable. That's when you'll want to look into a fulfillment house. They will take care of warehousing, packing, and shipping. Some of the fees involved include set-up fees, storage fees, order processing fees, return processing fees, and fees to receive merchandise. But the extra money you'll be paying will be worth it when you get to the point where you need to spend more time on sales and marketing and less time hauling stuff to the post office. Not to mention the time you'll spend waiting in line.

BUILDING WEBSITE LOYALTY:

Swiggies isn't really the kind of site that people would come back to over and over again, unless they were buying the electrolyte drink mix (read the section on consummables). If I wanted to get steady customers, I'd have to give them content. I'd have to give them something of value.

This is when I came up with kidfunruns.com. This site is a listing of all the kid's fun runs in the world. It also has valuable content for parents and kids that relates to the running community. Nothing is sold on the site. Just pure content. And, of course, a link to the swiggies site.

I also started a content site for movie reviews, hiddenvideogems.com. Again, it's not a product site, but it gives valuable information.

These sites take a lot of time, and you'll have to put a lot of work into them, but the point isn't to make money on them right away, although you might. You're building a portfolio. Your goal is to make money on them in the future and to keep growing your Money Garden. Your websites should be a constantly changing entity. Whenever you add valuable information to your site let everybody know.

Loyalty on the web is about building relationships. Are you helping to enrich the lives of your customers? Do they feel valued and respected? Try to understand the psychology behind what makes them tick and why they would go back to your website or your brand over others.

Even if your product is sold at a higher price, you can still gain customer loyalty. Price isn't necessarily the only thing people consider when making a purchase or becoming a loyal customer. Your long-term loyalty from customers must be earned. This takes time. You have to prove that you're trustworthy and dependable. Openly explain your privacy policy.

Let your visitors know that you don't intend to sell or rent their information to a third party.

Don't give customers what you want to give them. Give them what they want. And to find out what they want, just ask them. Personalize your reward program and make it harder for other companies to compete with it. Offer your customers gift certificates. You should offer them year-round and not just at Christmas.

Start an affiliate program for your own products so others can make money off of them. The easiest way is to pay an affiliate service program to track it and calculate the sales and do the accounting. Make sure it's worth the cost before starting it.

And lastly, build relationships with other websites so they will link to *your* site with backlinks. Backlinks are hyperlinks that link from a web page back to your own website. You need to have backlinks that are in line with the subject matter of your site. Good link popularity can dramatically increase traffic to your site. It can also increase your search engine rankings. You should be linked from every site that is of interest to your market.

TIPS ON WEB LINKS:

- Avoid linking to the "link farms", some of which have hundreds of outgoing links. Your page ranking can be negatively affected by these.
- Link to non-competing sites that are valuable to your customers. Send them a thank you after they do it. And offer to put their link on your site.

- Text links are more important to the search engines than graphical links. They are mixed in with the content of a page and are less intrusive than banner ads.
- Find out who your competitors are getting links from. If appropriate, also get the same sources to link to you. Search for "Google Webmaster Tools". They offer tools to show you the backlinks to a site.
- If you find a great website that you'd like to link to, contact them. It couldn't hurt to ask, and they might just say "yes".
- Avoid anything that will get you kicked off the search engines, such as using copyrighted or trademarked words in your META tags (a special HTML tag that stores information about a website, but isn't displayed in a web browser), adding keywords that don't have anything to do with your site, or adding multiple uses of the same word to your META tags.

Jen Bolter is a webmaster for a celebrity fan site called Rising Stars. I interviewed her about what business owners should expect from a web designer and how to make the relationship run smoothly:

What should business owners look for in a web designer?

It's important to find a web designer who cares about their clients and gets back to them in a timely manner. A web designer should also listen to what the client wants, and work with them to achieve their vision while creating a site that will accomplish their goals.

What are the costs involved in putting up a website?

The costs involved vary based on what you're looking for. Costs that can go into a website include: hosting costs, domain registration costs, and optional costs which can be applied to a domain name, including SSL certificates, domain verification, and whois privacy. A web designer can manage any or all of those things. With my experience, it's been half and half in regards to domain registration. About half of the clients handle registering their own domain name and extra domain options.

Do you handle the hosting?

As a web designer I handle the design, hosting, and maintenance of the websites.

What's the best way to work with a web designer? How can you make their job easier while saving time and money?

The best way to work with a web designer is through good communication. Make an outline of the exact way you want your site to look and show examples of existing sites.

What questions should a business owner ask before starting a website?

"What are the costs of your services?" "Does your cost include maintenance?" "Could I see some examples of other websites you've done?"

Who needs a website?

Anyone who wants to make their company, product, art, service, or non-profit visible to a local or global audience needs a website. It's a great promotional tool for businesses and a great tool for celebrities to keep in contact with their fan base.

BLOGS

Blogs were originally called web logs on simple web pages that were read like diaries in reverse date order. In fact, many are still like online diaries. The blog on the website for this book www.createforcash.com, is basically the diary of an entrepreneur.

The way I started this book in the first place was by taking notes every day about what I learned by doing everything myself. My blog is an inside look at what an entrepreneur goes through every day. The good days, the bad days, and the "pull your hair out by the roots" days.

Today, blogs are used as an adjunct to a regular website or business. Actors and musicians have websites that are read by their fans. Business owners use them to keep in touch with customers and create income through ad sales and affiliate links. Schools use blogging for educational purposes. Many people build up a successful blog only to sell it down the road.

A blog can also be a stand-alone business, where you provide unique, interesting content, and make money with advertising (such as Google Ad Sense) and selling related products directly or through affiliate links. The best known is through Amazon.com. Some bloggers actually make quite a good income just from blogging.

But, blogging for a living isn't for the impatient. It takes time to build up a blog that makes money. But don't let that stop you from adding a blog to your Money Garden. Just like a regular garden, a Money Garden also takes time to grow.

Bloggers can write about niche markets that target an audience that regular journalists employed by the mainstream media can't. Blogs are attractive to the search engines because they are constantly adding content on a regular basis. You can also stay in touch with your readers if they subscribe to your blog. This way they receive blog updates from you automatically.

You need to ask yourself if blogging is something you could actually do every single day. The first time I tried it, I was really gung-ho at first, and then I ran out of steam. This happens to a lot of people after the initial excitement wears off. Make sure you can keep it up. And, if you can keep it up, do a blog for each business in your Money Garden. (You have multiple talents, right?)

It's better to have separate blogs for each topic anyway. The more you can narrow down your niche, the better. Search engines like Google tend to favor a topic that is well defined.

Put some thought into what your audience wants to know about. If you sell cookware, your customers may want to hear about new recipes or tips on how to cook a gourmet meal on a budget. You can give them information on cooking, but you can also review new cookware, interview a well-known chef, or create a debate between two chefs with differing opinions.

Blogs can be interactive with comments from your readers, which adds material to your blog. You may, however, want to create boundaries on what is acceptable.

You can also add content by having contests. On kidsfun-runs.com, I do product reviews and have contests. Contestants are required to go to the sponsor's website and answer a question before they can enter. You can determine the winner by a random drawing, then post the winners on your blog.

You can also put surveys and polls on your blog. It will give you a better idea of who is reading it and what they want to know about. Survey Monkey is one easy to use tool for creating surveys.

Besides making money directly from a blog, you can make money indirectly from a blog by building up credibility, using it to showcase your writing, or by using it to get speaking engagements and consulting jobs.

You can put ads on your blogs from the beginning or wait until you have more of an audience. Ads could either be in the form of banners, text links, sponsorships, Amazon product ads or Google Ad Sense. Make sure you have the right balance of advertising. Enough to make money, but not so much that it turns off your audience. They are there for the content.

You can also join a blog network to pick up readership faster. The ad revenue is split, but because of search engine placement and increased traffic, it could bring in more than you would on your own. The downside of joining a network is a question of ownership rights. Make sure you know who owns the rights to the blog and what happens to them if you decide to leave the network.

Provide valuable content on a consistent basis and keep plugging your blog any way you can, online and off.

Researching the market

This is going to seem like common sense, but researching the market is always a must. Before you embark on any new business endeavors you need to see what's out there. If there is competition, how can you do it better? One of the first places to start looking is on the Internet.

Before you start your business:

- Do a basic search to see if your idea is already out there. To search for patents, go to Google and click on advanced search, then click on "more", then ""even more", and you'll find "patent search".
- Do some research on new products in the search engines. Something may be out there that isn't patented.
- Do a search on your topics to see what's out there. Try every combination of keywords.
- Take a trip to the mall. Go in every store and check out what's on the shelves. Go to the local drug store, grocery store, mom and pop stores, neighborhood flea markets. Find out what people are selling.
- Look through every catalog you can find that might possibly carry your product. Look through credit card inserts.
- What kind of products are being shown on QVC, HSN, or as an infomercial?
- Keep up with current affairs. Read and watch the news. What kind of trends can you spot?

Continued next page

Before you start your business:

- What are the trends in a particular industry? Look through trade magazines and wholesale magazines to see what new products are on the market.
- Walk as many trade shows as you can. Sometimes they won't let you do it, but if you can, walk the show first before committing to a booth and check out what's there. Are any of the products or services there your competition? Or is there anyone there you can network with?

PUT IT INTO ACTION

- ☐ Start creating your brand name
- ☐ Lock up domains with your brand name
- ☐ Research similar service companies in your area
- ☐ Write down all of the ways you could act as a middleman
- ☐ Brainstorm unique events that relate to your business

CHAPTER

5

Planting the Seeds

"Drive thy business or it will drive you."
—BENJAMIN FRANKLIN

Now that you've researched the market, decided on your topic, created products and services to sell and how you're going to use your skills to sell them, you need to get the word out there.

Remember to do it in this order and don't start spending money you don't have yet:

- Marketing for Free
- Marketing Cheap
- Marketing with Money

Usually the first thing most people think of is advertising. But, in my opinion, that's the very last thing you should use.

Imagine for a minute that you have absolutely no money to spend, but yet you have to get the word out about your great business. What would you do? This is what I was faced with when I started my first business. Zero marketing dollars. I had to get very creative. It's this creativity that will probably set your business apart from others. You have to stand out in a crowd, and it's a challenge to do that with no money. But this is where you'll learn the most.

I manufactured just enough product to get started and then I took my swiggies down to the beach. I put them on and drank out of them while I intentionally looked people in the eye so they would feel comfortable approaching me. I never used any kind of hard sales tactics and waited for them to make a move. If they were interested, they would stop me and ask where I got them. I had a whole knapsack full of them in all colors. If they bought two or more they got a discount. And they almost always did.

I started thinking if *I* could sell them that easily, I bet other people could sell them too. But where would I find those people? I made a really primitive flyer and put tear-offs at the bottom with my phone number on it. Then I put the flyers on every bulletin board I could find, especially near gyms and colleges. Soon I was getting others out selling like I was. So the first free marketing strategy I tried was direct sales.

DIRECT SALES & MARKETING

Although not actual sales, the first trade in history was barter. Early civilizations exchanged pottery for ivory, or stone vessels for ebony. The first direct sellers were the peddlers, merchants and traders who traveled on foot, on donkeys, or by caravan to sell their wares to people on their travels. The purchase price was usually higher than the typical trading centers because of the hazards involved and the convenience for the buyer.

The direct sellers used the trading centers as a stopping point on their journeys. To them it was another way of making sales. These early direct sellers knew how to take advantage of selling opportunities.

Religious feasts were gathering places for armies in the field. The direct seller would sell them items they needed. Some followed the armies on the march. They also sold flowers and fruit on street corners, a practice that can be traced back as early as the fourteenth century. This practice is still flourishing today.

Worldwide economic expansion started around the tenth century. The direct seller played an important role during the Commercial Revolution of the tenth to thirteenth centuries. Early settlers traveled by horse-drawn wagon peddling their wares from town to town. Some of them doubled as performers, fortune-tellers, and healers. Those were the ones who knew the value of up-sales! Some of the goods they sold then included pots and pans, scissors, combs, horses, and the local news.

One of the best salesmen around, Ron Popeil, started the very same way. As a kid he hawked everything from pots and pans to shoeshine spray on a Chicago street corner and would later go on to become an infomercial icon.

Door-to-door sales became popular in the 1920's when a boom of labor-saving devices were invented that appealed to the housewife. Electric irons, washing machines, and vacuum cleaners sold like hotcakes to women who were fed up with the drudgery of time-consuming and labor-intensive chores.

When the economic downturns came, door-to-door companies actually did quite well since there were more willing recruits who canvassed more territories.

Some companies used this type of selling to introduce their new products, which were later sold into the retail stores. The modern equivalent would be the use of infomercials to reach consumers, which in turn drive sales in retail.

Two of the most popular direct sales companies, Fuller Brush and Avon, are still going strong today. These companies gave opportunities to people who might not otherwise be able to make the kind of money they could make in sales. You don't need a college degree, and the sky's the limit as to how much money you want to make.

If you need any inspiration, watch the movie "Door to Door" about saleman Bill Porter. For years he was told that he was unemployable because he had cerebral palsy, until he started working for the Watkins Company. Year after tear he won "Salesman of the Year" and proved everyone wrong.

If direct selling appeals to you, consider becoming a walking/driving billboard. Instead of advertising other brands, advertise your own. Wear your brand on T-shirts and hats. Put your brand on a car magnet, license plate cover, and any other way you can show it off.

I'm planning on turning an old van into a swiggiemobile. Look in the parking lot at a trade show and see how many vans have been turned into a moving advertisement for their business. It's like a moving billboard without the cost. And it doubles as a way to haul your stuff around to shows.

Carry around business cards and brochures with your brand. You never know who you'll meet. For me, it was easy. I just wore swiggies and people would always ask. Have your 10–30 second elevator speech prepared in case someone asks what *you* do.

HOME PARTIES

By the 1950s the home party became another form of direct sales. It allowed people to demonstrate their wares and it was also a great way to socialize.

Some of the most successful home party companies include Tupperware and Mary Kay Cosmetics. Another one, The Pampered Chef, is one of the most successful companies of its kind. Founded by Doris Christopher in the basement of her Chicago home, it was eventually acquired by Berkshire Hathaway. It's now the largest direct seller of housewares in the U.S., with more than 67,000 "Kitchen Consultant" sales reps.

Some of the more unique businesses include Taser and Botox parties. What kind of unique direct selling parties can you think of?

CARTS AND KIOSKS

Another form of direct selling that is increasing in popularity is the cart/kiosk business. Cart owners sell everything from unique gift items to food. You'll find carts and kiosks in malls, train stations, airports, hospitals, sports arenas, and for special events like festivals or parades.

Wherever you decide to set up your cart, one of the most important factors in your success will be the location. Choose a good high traffic area.

Vending carts come in a variety of sizes and each one is custom-built. If you're going to work in a mall you might want to check with the mall management to see if they will lease you a cart. Most malls also will want to approve the layout of the cart and how the merchandise is displayed.

If you want to operate your cart from a mall you'll need to fill out an application from the management office. It can take several months to be approved and set up your business, so plan ahead.

The advantage of running your business from a cart or kiosk is a much lower cost of entry. While a permanent retail location can cost hundreds of thousands of dollars and long lease times, a cart or kiosk can offer you the flexibility of starting inexpensively and leasing for shorter time periods, allowing you to test the waters at different locations.

You'll need to have the appropriate business licenses and permits before you can open your cart business. If you sell food you'll need a health or food permit from your county, city, or state health department. Also, some states require food handlers to pass a food handling course.

Seasonal products tend to work well with a cart business. Examples would be gift baskets before Christmas or sports franchise items during football or baseball season. Since timing is critical, make sure you allow plenty of time for delivery of your inventory.

TRADE SHOWS

Trade shows are similar to flea markets in that you have a booth/storefront, but you are usually selling to buyers instead of the public. And they are much more expensive to exhibit at, with some costing as much as several thousands of dollars for a booth.

You are also usually only selling your own products or ones from other people that you want to rep or distribute.

Always try to walk a trade show, if you can, before plunking down a lot of money for a booth. I made this mistake when I registered for something called the Action Sports Retailer Show. I thought, "Okay, this sounds like it would be right for my product". And boy was I wrong!

As soon as the customers started filing in I knew I was in the wrong place. People with purple mohawks and multiple piercings cruised the aisles looking for skateboards and surfboards. Nothing against people with purple mohawks, but it wasn't even close to being my target market. Not only that, but my booth was practically in the parking lot, next to the skateboard ramp. The music was so loud I couldn't even carry on a conversation with the people in the next booth, who were also quite upset.

Before the end of the day, I went to the head office in tears. I had spent the last dime I had on that show and it was a total bust. They agreed to give me my money back. But the lesson I learned was to make sure the show is exactly targeted to your market, and don't assume because it says "sports" in the title that it's the right sports show for you.

Surprisingly, that show was one of the best things that happened to me because I met a guy there who sold in the promotional market. He was also in the wrong show, so we both had plenty of time to talk since neither one of us had any customers. He became a friend, and helped mentor me in how to sell to the promotional market.

The lesson here is that no matter what show you're at, milk it to the fullest. Don't just sit in your booth. Get out and network. Network with people in other booths, with the press, with customers . . . everybody. You never know who you'll meet or what kind of opportunities could come your way.

HERE ARE SOME HELPFUL TIPS FOR TRADESHOW SUCCESS:

- Get there early and walk the whole show. You can learn a lot by studying other booths. What makes you want to stop?
- Have a nice banner sign over the top or the back of your booth. Make sure you use pictures that instantly show what you have for sale. Step away from your booth and walk as far away as possible. Can you still see your sign? Does it catch your attention? Do you instantly understand what the product is?
- Pretend you're a customer and see what they see. Your booth looks different when you're standing in it. Quickly walk past your own booth. Does anything in it make you want to stop?

- Have a drawing for a prize. Nothing gets people to stop like free stuff. That way you also capture their email information. Or have some kind of skill contest. Or . . . there's always face painting.
- A good rule of thumb for pricing at a trade show is to take your cost and add 40%, and don't forget to charge sales tax.
- Even though you shouldn't use it, you might want to have a chair. I would never recommend sitting for any length of time. You simply don't have the same kind of energy, and you don't want customers to think you're not interested in their business.
- Greet every one of your customers as they walk by. You want them to be as excited as you are. Unless, of course, you get a mean "Leave me alone" kind of look. You'll also learn by the end of the day to dole out your energy sparingly. You'll start to develop a sixth sense about who to "pitch" to. They'll let you know.
- Bring someone with you if you can. I usually work shows by myself, but it's more fun if you have a partner. You'll need the breaks, and it helps pass the time if it gets slow.
- Don't forget to bring enough change and a credit card swiper. Once I learned that, I ended up selling about twice as much. People will run out of cash, but they'll usually have their credit card with them. Don't give them a reason not to buy.
- Bring your own food and drinks. If you buy everything at the show it gets a bit expensive.

- Dress professionally, but comfortably. You want to make a good first impression and you never know who might stop by your booth.

- Wear nice, comfortable shoes. You'll probably be standing all day, and no one will see your feet anyway.

- Make sure you have plenty of business cards, flyers and catalogs. Also, take a stack of press kits. Most trade shows have a press room. Always look for it the day you start setting up your booth and leave plenty of press kits there.

- Bring a variety of office supplies, like pens, notebooks, tape, scissors, etc.

- Set up a video of your press, commercials, and interviews. Keep it small and keep the volume low. People will be attracted to the visual.

- Get several other companies together for a roundtable discussion about an important industry topic after hours at a trade show. Go around to several booths and ask if they want to participate. Rent a conference room and tape the discussion. Then contact a trade magazine about using it in their next publication. It's a great article for their readers and great PR for all of the companies involved. Plus it's another way to network in an intimate setting with other companies. Invite some members of the press to sit in on it and serve coffee and snacks. Make sure you prepare some questions beforehand because you will be doing the moderating.

FLEA MARKETS, FAIRS, & FESTIVALS

If you think flea markets are only for people selling used goods, think again. Most flea markets now sell new and used merchandise. In fact, some of the most successful vendors sell new merchandise. I've done quite well selling at flea markets. And the more I worked them, the more I learned.

There's something exciting about having your own booth/storefront and interacting with hundreds or thousands of people. It's one of the best ways I've found to learn how to sell, and also to find out about your own products firsthand from your target audience. You get instant feedback.

I went to a kids fair to get the kid's swiggies brand out there in front of the parents and kids. For three days I was barely able to take a break. Yes, eight straight hours on your feet is a bit much, but it's also exhilarating when you're selling like crazy. And I didn't even have face painting. (Hint: Kids LOVE face painting.)

I've met people at flea markets who travel around from show to show or just work on the weekends and make a killing. Well, by a killing, I mean $500 or more a day. But that's a nice chunk of change for a weekend job. And it's fun. The great thing about flea markets is that you can exhibit at them for very little money.

Unless you have at least a dozen of your own products to sell, you'll need to sell things from others also. I made the mistake in the beginning of only having one product. Give your customers choices. Also, if people buy one thing from you, and they like you and your stuff, they will buy more. Give them more. You already have a booth anyway, so sell as much as you can and make it worthwhile.

There are plenty of places to find wholesale products on the Internet. Be creative. Sell something unique that you can't find in stores. You can usually find some great buys at close-out companies since you'll be buying in large volume. Good products for flea markets are inexpensive and are impulse buys. Have products at three different price points. Most people will buy at the middle price, but if they're tight on funds or feel like splurging, with a low end and high priced product, you will have them covered.

I would always sell one set of swiggies at one price and two for a discounted price. Usually most people buy two sets. After all, they make great, unique gifts, so buying a second set for someone else makes sense. Don't forget to mention that. Most people won't be thinking that far ahead. Help them see the possibilities. People shopping at a flea market are looking for bargains. Your margins may be smaller, but you should make up for that with volume.

Make your booth space your own. You'll get very little time to catch someone's attention who is walking by, so make sure your booth stands out. Have your merchandise in displays like you'd find at a retail store. You can buy off-the-shelf displays that fit your products, so make your setup as professional as you can.

Direct Mail

Direct mail is when a message is sent directly to the consumer through the mail system. The purpose is usually to target a specific demographic group.

Mail order began around the time of the invention of the typewriter in 1867. The first modern mail order catalog was produced by Montgomery Ward in 1872. In Europe, direct mail can be traced all the way back to the fifteenth century and the invention of movable type.

Marketers tend to like direct mail because they get rapid feedback. If they send out a thousand pieces of mail and get responses from a hundred, they immediately know if it works or not, as opposed to a commercial that you can't track. It's also a great way to test ads to see which ones pull the best. With direct mail, your message doesn't have to compete with anyone else. It's the only ad on the page.

The post office has lower rates for buyers of bulk mail permits. In order to qualify, the mail must be sorted in a specific way. Although some people react negatively to direct mail, many actually respond positively since the message is targeted to their demographic, and they are able to find useful goods and services this way. The message is personalized to them.

Some of the formats include:

■ Self-mailers: Ads from a single sheet that have been printed and folded. There is usually a message on the outside to get your attention enough to open it up.

- Clear bag packages: Large, full-color packages in a clear, outer wrap.
- Postcards: A simple two-sided piece with a message on one side and the customer's address on the other.
- Envelope mailers: Pieces where the marketing material is placed inside an envelope. With this type you can include more than one piece.

Yes, it's easier to market on the Internet, but nothing beats hitting your target market like sending a well-timed postcard directly to someone else's mailbox. And they don't have to find you. You find them. You can time it perfectly with specific sales and promotions. You don't have any middlemen. The message is personal and directed only to them with products and services they may be looking for.

You can get very specific about who you want to target with your mailing. On one mailing, I was only targeting women between the ages of twenty-five and fifty, and only women who were interested in selling fitness products in their spare time. That's pretty specific.

Direct mail can help create marketing synergy. Use it to get the word out about your website. A website is like a sign in the desert if nobody knows about it. And a great way to let everyone know about it is by cross promoting your site with your offline direct mail campaign.

Several ways to use direct mail include:

- Notifying customers of new products or services
- Private sales

- Special events
- Reminders
- Discount offers
- Keeping in touch with existing customers
- Testing different types of ads
- Driving traffic to a website

You should build interest in your product or service, but make sure you have some kind of call to action, like a special offer for a limited time, or they will put off making the call. Take away the risk and make it easy for them to order. Include an 800 number and your website for more information. Sell the customer on what's in it for them. Get right to the point and tell them how your product or service will help them.

Postcards

I think one of the most successful types of direct mail is the postcard. It's simple, inexpensive, and you can't miss the message. It's in your mailbox staring you in the face, and almost all of them get read. I'm surprised that so few people use them. But that's what makes them stand out as a great marketing technique.

Some advantages are:

- Postcards are relatively inexpensive to print up and cost a third less to mail than a regular letter.
- You don't have to open an envelope to see the message. It's right there. That's why you need to have a catchy ad that grabs you, that's simple to read and not cluttered

with too much copy. Create a powerful headline that generates curiosity.

- You can put different codes on different postcards to track which ones work and where the sale came from. Give your postcard customers a special discount.
- Postcards can be mailed, but they can also be used to get your message out at trade shows or posted on bulletin boards. Use them instead of business cards.
- Postcards don't have spam filters like emails do. Use them before a phone call or as an introduction before sending an email.
- Postcards are most effective when used to generate sales leads or to drive traffic to your website. They don't contain enough information to close a sale, just enough to generate interest and get them to your site for more information.

Figure out exactly what you want your postcards to accomplish. And figure out what you want the customer to do. Don't waste the opportunity. Make the message on your cards a friendly message and not a hard-core sales pitch. Use a big, bold headline and keep the copy short. Use bullet points so you can read it easily. Address the cards yourself if you can and use real stamps. The more personal the touch, the better the results will be.

A postcard marketing campaign should be repetitive. Mail them out every two to three weeks or more. The results you'll get will make up for the frequency. People need to see your message more than once.

BROCHURES & FLYERS

If you want to tell more of your business's story, you can do it with brochures. You can use brochures in a direct mail campaign and you can also hand them out, like postcards, at trade shows, in crowded areas, or through other businesses.

Helpful hints for using brochures and flyers:

- Put your flyers on community bulletin boards, libraries, waiting rooms, recreational facilities, colleges, churches, street corners, under car windshield wipers and any other public place where it's legal to do so.
- Hand out flyers on a busy street corner. Target the customers you think would be interested in your business.
- Find a good printer and graphic designer to work with you to create the best possible direct mail piece. Make sure you check for spelling and grammar before printing. You want to show that your business has credibility.
- Check to make sure all of the facts are correct, and your prices are up to date. This is going to sound like common sense, but make sure all of your information, including company name, website and phone number, is on the postcard or flyer. (I made this costly mistake once!)
- Your direct mail piece should catch their attention with an easy to read type style, bullet points, comments, underlining, bold type, capitals, and an intriguing format. It should be entertaining without detracting

from the message. Use short words and short sentences. Use the word *you* a lot. Be concise and to the point.

USING MAILING LISTS:

Once you have your direct mail pieces, you'll need to have a list to send them to. Of course the best list will always be your own. Again, I made this mistake in the beginning of my swiggies business. I thought since I only had one product I didn't need to save my customers emails. But I can't tell you how many people asked me if I had anything else to sell. Well, I didn't then. But I have since gotten a little wiser and expanded my product line. Now I wish I had kept the emails.

As long as you sell a great product and have great service, there is always the chance that your customers will want to buy from you again. Your most recent customers will be your best prospects.

The next best lists would be response lists. These are rented or sold by other businesses and are hand-picked because the names on the list have already shown interest in your subject or they have bought from the other similar business.

You need to find out as much as you can about the list you will be using. Have the people actually bought before? How long ago? How often did they buy or respond? If they bought, how big was the order? Are the addresses accurate? Do they give credit for incorrect addresses?

Narrow your target as much as possible by demographic and socioeconomic characteristics. If you're going to rent a list, the terms are almost always for a one time use only.

Any responders can be re-mailed again without further rental charges.

Lists are valuable and list owners will protect their lists by adding their own names, but with a different spelling, so they can check up on their renters and make sure they're not violating the rules.

One of the best reasons to use direct mail is that you can easily test it. It allows you to see if your advertising and marketing message is hitting the mark. Test your campaign by slowly changing just one element of your direct mail piece at a time. This will eventually narrow your marketing campaign down so that you will be able to save more money in the future. And you'll get a great ad that really works.

Be sure to test your list first to make sure you are getting to the right customers. Then you'll want to test your offer. Are they responding to your free seminar or free gift? And how many sales did you close from that?

Which postcard or flyer style did they like the best? And was the timing of the piece accurate? Did it help to send it every two weeks? Did you get a better response by sending the postcard or the flyer? Try different combinations of the above. And keep testing.

More tips on using direct mail:

- If you're going to advertise, your direct mail should be timed to be received just after the ad runs.
- Send out 2,000 pieces five times a year instead of 10,000 all at once.

- Keep good records and keep track of how much you spend on each mailing. Also, keep track of your split runs to see which ads are working. (A split ad is where you send one ad to half of your list and a different ad to the other half.)

- Cross promote by including an advertisement from another one of your products in each order that you ship out. When they receive your package, they might be in the mood to order something else. And, like I said, if people like you and like doing business with you, they will keep ordering from you.

- People are more likely to read your direct mail piece if they think they're going to get something out of it. Yes, people are always thinking "What's in it for me?" Sell them on the benefits to them first, and the product features second.

- Include testimonials and guarantees. Make it exclusive. ("Not sold in stores.") Have some kind of urgency in it. ("Free shipping for the first 30 customers".)

- Make it easy for your customers to respond. Include postage paid replies, include an 800 number, have check off boxes, etc.

John Schulte, President of the National Mail Order Association fills us in on "How to Make Direct Mail Work for You":

Methods of using direct mail

Direct mail is used in many ways. You can sell a product or service, generate leads for salesmen, create foot traffic at a retail store, remind people of something, keep your name in a customer's mind, conduct surveys for customer input. How many different ones have you been sent? Oil change. Dentist checkup. Happy birthday from insurance agent or restaurant.

The direct mail strategy

The first step in planning a direct mail campaign is to think about the objective of your mailing. What is the reason for making the mailing? Are you trying to get orders by mail? Produce more sales leads? Sell subscriptions? Raise funds by mail? Entice customers to visit a store? Once we clearly understand the objective we have a better chance of success.

Remember, with all direct mail advertising you must be able to fulfill your backend. If you solicit leads for salesmen, salesmen must be in place. Leads must be followed up at once. Don't be caught unprepared.

The components of the classic direct mail package

The sales letter, a brochure or circular, an order form, a return envelope. In most cases, a lift letter is used ("only read this if you decide not to buy", "a message from the editor"). Also, often included is a free gift slip.

What is your offer and how should you present it?

An offer is simply the way you present what you are selling to your prospect or customer. In other words, what will the recipient get if they take the action you ask them to take in your mailing? In our opinion the offer is the second most important element of using direct mail successfully. Who you send it to is number one. Why is the offer important? Because it can mean the difference between the success and failure of a mailing. Because it can make a successful mailing even more successful.

What does an offer include?

Your product or service, the price, the payment terms, any incentives you're willing to throw in (like a free gift) and any special conditions attached to the offer.

Constantly work on the mailer and the way it's presented. Since direct mail advertising can be measured exactly, the effectiveness of one versus another can be scientifically tested to find out what works best using split run testing. This is done by having every other name on the list receive the same mailing with only the offer changed. Make sure you code the response device.

The more attractive you can make your offer, the better the response will be. You want an offer that will make people take action right away. So your goal is to come up with a very attractive offer with high perceived value, but low cost to you. Many times the best offer won't be the most expensive, but could be literature or booklets.

Your objective is to increase response by more than enough to offset the added costs involved, so that your cost-per-order is lower than it was without the free gift.

The Direct Mail letter

The most important component in any direct mail package is the letter. Crafting a good letter is a skill that has to be practiced. Every word, sentence and paragraph has a reason for being there. There's no such thing as a letter that's too long . . . only too boring. Here is a formula for writing a direct mail letter.

- Get attention
- Arouse interest
- Stimulate desire
- Build confidence
- Ask for action

Attention: Getting attention is the most important. The way to get your prospect's attention is with your headline. The first words should shout out and flag down those people who would be most interested in what you have to offer. The second thing your headline should contain is the benefit the reader is going to get from reading your letter or ad.

Interest: You should have already gotten their interest by stating a big benefit in your headline. Now the opening paragraph has the floor. This is where you must grab the reader and not let go. Do this by listing more and more benefits. Put the strongest benefits first. By the time the reader gets through the first few paragraphs they are fully interested in what you're saying. Now they want to know more.

Desire: You have their full attention. Now create the desire to own whatever it is you're selling. You have already sold them on all the benefits they will receive. Show them how your product or service will provide those benefits.

Confidence: Now is the time to convince your reader to fully trust you and your claims. You can do this with the help of testimonials and a risk-free offer that puts all the risk on your shoulders.

Action: Time to make your prospect an irresistible offer to try your products or services. Make the offer even better if they act NOW. Walk them through the buying process.

To recap, here is the seven step formula for writing a direct mail sales letter:

1. Promise a benefit in your first paragraph or headline
2. Immediately enlarge on your most important benefit
3. Tell the reader specifically what he or she is going to get
4. Back up your statements with proof and endorsements
5. Tell the reader what he or she will lose if they don't act
6. Re-phrase your prominent benefits in your closing offer
7. Incite action NOW by restating a benefit or adding a free gift

Direct mail campaigns are always changing. Until you find just the right combination, you change one thing at a time until you find out what produces the most profits.

Infomercials

Infomercials really took off around 1984 when the FCC eliminated regulations that governed the commercial content of television. Infomercials are direct response TV commercials that can be anywhere from 30 seconds to a half-hour long. They are either short form or long form.

For the purpose of this book, you will probably never shoot a long form infomercial spot unless you are heavily financed. But a one minute short form can be shot for less than $10,000. My short form swiggies spot was actually shot for less and was done by a well-known film director in Los Angeles.

It's not the infomercial that costs so much, it's the air time. But if you're lucky enough to get some P.I. (per inquiry) advertising, you can bring those costs down quite a bit. Per Inquiry advertising is where a TV station will make a commission agreement with you so you pay them a flat amount for each order you generate. This is a last resort for the station and they only do it if they have leftover ad time that doesn't sell.

You can also use the spot at trade shows and on your website to show your product in action. You'll want to test your infomercial on local broadcast and national cable channels to see how it works. If you have a hit, then it will go into "roll-out" nationally.

Infomercials are now used to drive retail traffic, with some just breaking even on television. Studies show most people will make their decisions by watching the infomercial, but will buy the product at the retail store. Infomercial products should be unique and appear to be an incredible value. "But wait . . . there's more!" Your ratio of sales price to cost of goods should be at least five to one and the product should have mass-market appeal. It's helpful to have a product that's an impulse buy and shows well on television. It should have a good story and solve a problem.

Marty Fahncke of Fawn Key and Associates gives some advice on how the entrepreneur can make an infomercial work:

What kind of products work best in an infomercial?

The best infomercial products solve a problem or fill a need, are demonstrable, and have a great "before and after" story. That's why you see so many fitness, weight loss, business opportunity, and beauty and cooking products. With products in each of these categories you can clearly see the before and after benefit with a skinnier body, easy to cook food, and money in the bank. It also helps if the product is truly innovative and unique to the marketplace. There is an old saying in marketing "You can never be too young, too thin, or too rich". Develop a product which answers one of these and you're on your way to a winner!

What kind of products don't work?

- Products that don't show a clear result.
- Products without the proper margin to make it on TV (in today's expensive media environment, you should have at minimum a 5:1 mark-up, and an 8:1 mark-up or better is even more desirable).
- Products which are too difficult to explain, or appear too difficult for the customer to use.

Can you explain the difference between short form and long form, and how do you know which one to use?

- A short form infomercial is generally 60 seconds in length, although you will occasionally see a 30 second or a 2 minute. This length is good if you have a product that is simple to demonstrate, and the benefits of the product are easy to understand. Simple kitchen gadgets, diet products, and other easy to understand products fit this type of media. One other factor is price point. Generally a product priced higher than $39.95 does not do well in short form, as there is simply not enough time to build the value in that short time frame. The best price point for a short form infomercial is $19.95.
- A long form is 28:30 in length, though it is generally called a half-hour, even though it falls short by a minute and a half. This format is desirable

if you have a complex product with lots of benefits. It allows you a lot more time to showcase customer testimonials, which can be one of the most powerful marketing tools in direct response TV. Half-hour infomercials also allow you enough time to tell a story in order to build value, so price points are less of an issue. Products selling for hundreds or even thousands of dollars can be sold via long form half-hour infomercials.

Is there a way to test an infomercial for very little money to see if it will work?

Absolutely! Three ways to test infomercials are:

1. Online video—you can create the video and promote it on YouTube and other video sites. The response rates from that can often give you an idea of how an infomercial will do on TV.
2. Online marketing—we've found that doing online marketing, such as email marketing and search engines can be a great way to test a number of variables before spending a ton of money launching on TV. We're able to test headlines, copy, offer structure, price points, upsells, and many other variables before ever spending a dime on TV. That way when we do move forward with a big DRTV budget, we know exactly what the market will respond to in order to make the sales come in.
3. Google TV Advertising—using Google TV Advertising you can test your infomercial with a very small budget, yet air your ad on local TV stations across the country. It can be highly targeted, and you can get started for as little as a few hundred dollars.

Why do retailers insist that you have an infomercial running before they will take your product? And can you get around that?

Retailers like to see "As Seen On TV" products because they know that for every ONE item sold on TV, SEVEN will be sold at retail. That's a lot of customers coming in to the store looking for the latest, greatest infomercial product. And, it's something for you, the product owner to keep in mind as you are mapping out your marketing plan and budget. However, having a product on TV is not a requirement to get into retail. Thousands of new products are placed at retail every year without being on TV first.

Fawnkey and Associates is a product development, marketing and consulting company which helps emerging and existing businesses increase revenue, profitability, and customer satisfaction through the use of integrated marketing and sales efforts.

Online Advertising

Online advertising costs much less than traditional advertising and can target your market just as well as offline advertising. You can also track your responses, and you can measure your success with most online advertising. Web traffic analysis software can tell you whether or not your ad was clicked on and if the customers went to that site, and how long they stayed there. If an ad doesn't perform as expected, this will allow you to either stop advertising on that site or to change your ads for better response.

You can use online advertising to drive traffic, but you can also use it to generate leads and build brand awareness.

Graphical ads, classified ads, sponsorships, and directory listings are the main forms of advertising online. There are free and paid classified ads online. They are easy to create and hit a target market. In a classified ad, you are targeting a customer who is already shopping. When you first post a classified ad it will appear at the top of the list. But as more ads are posted, your ad moves down the list. It can very quickly disappear from sight. If you want to keep it near the top, you'll have to keep re-submitting it, but you'll have to give the ad a different title. If you've submitted a free classified ad, it may disappear completely in a few days, due to lack of space or a very busy site. Check it weekly to make sure it's still there.

You can also find topic-specific ads in many forums and discussion groups, such as AOL's Business Strategies. These are usually free and tend to target the people who will be the most interested in reading them. You can also advertise your content site and "sell" them once they get there. But by offering them free valuable information, you might have a better chance of getting them to go to that site.

Make your classified ad titles stand out. Use powerful words to catch the attention of your readers. Pose your title as a question. For example, "How much is your junk worth?" "Tired of paying too much for car insurance?" Be specific about what is that you're selling. "Wrist water bottle". "All-natural, sugar-free electrolyte drink mix". Use different codes or key words to track the best ads.

Using Banner Ads:

- Make sure your banner ad loads quickly and is easy to read. Make sure it doesn't link to an error page by ensuring it links to the appropriate page on your site. You can have a static, rotating, animated, or scrolling banner ads.
- Banner ads should be placed on content sites that reflect what it is you are selling. Use a banner ad to sell a product and not your website. When you click on a banner ad, it should take you to the page where that particular product is sold, not to your homepage where they'll have to search around to place an order.
- Use an expanding banner ad. An expanding banner ad looks like a regular banner ad, but expands when you click on it. Some of them actually let you order directly from the banner ad without leaving the site you're on. Some banners have embedded HTML that allows you to use a drop-down menu that takes you directly to the page you want.

- If you don't have the budget to pay to put your banner ads on other sites, then the best solution is to exchange banner ads with another site. You put their ad on your site in exchange for an ad on their site.
- You can also sponsor a mailing list or a newsletter. You can sponsor it by the day, week or month. Your sponsor ad will be prominently displayed and will target the readers of that list.

Google & Yahoo

Google advertising is one of the best types of online advertising you can do. You can advertise with Google AdWords or make money from others advertising on your site with Google AdSense.

You can control the Google AdWords budget by telling Google how much you're willing to pay per click and per day. You reach your target audience who is actively looking for the products and services you sell. Your AdWords appear on the same page as search results using your chosen keywords or on content sites in the Google network.

Submit your products to Froogle to be included in this price comparison search engine which was started by Google. Also, set up a pay-per-click account with Yahoo! Search Marketing. Yahoo! and Google dominate most of the market. With Yahoo! you're also listing with their many partner sites.

Watch out for click fraud—people clicking to your account who have no intention of buying. Search engines are pretty good at spotting this, but unethical competitors could be behind it. Check discussion boards and pay attention to unusual click patterns, such as a sharp increase in queries with no sales.

You may not get rich selling your own ad space on your site, but every bit counts. Most advertisers are looking for high traffic content sites. You'll need to supply them with statistics about your site and how many visitors you get.

You need to have the technology to host banner ads. You'll also need to be able to keep track of the number of visitors so you know how much to charge them for the ad space.

eBay

eBay calls itself "the world's largest online marketing place—where practically anyone can sell practically anything at anytime". It's business is virtual, self-regulating, and globally far-reaching. And it's a business where the market determines the cost of goods. There is also an eBay social network within the site where eBay members can chat, blog, and join others in group discussions.

EBay's community values basically believes that its members should be honest and fair in their dealings with others. The members are partially "regulated" by a feedback rating system. When customers buy or sell a product they are asked to give feedback about the transaction. The eBay community builds up a feedback profile over time. This is important, as it will help other buyers and sellers evaluate whether they want to do business with you or not.

Skip McGrath is highly regarded as one of the most knowledgeable eBay consultants around. He gives a few of his 77 tips to selling on eBay:

1. **Buy on eBay before you start trying to sell.**

   I get email from people all the time wanting to know how to make money selling on eBay. The first question I ask them is if they have ever bought anything on eBay. Amazingly a lot of them say "no". You really need to buy on eBay first to understand how the platform works and what eBay looks like from the buyer's point of view. You will never be successful on eBay until you learn how to buy.

2. **Learn to sell on eBay by selling on eBay.**

   The best way to start selling on eBay is to start selling on eBay. Yes, there are some things to learn. Take your time, look at the eBay help files (and these tips) and just start selling. You will make some mistakes—we all do. But don't get frustrated or give up. You will get better with experience. Also, selling will make you a better buyer. You will understand things from the seller's point of view and learn other ways to spot bargains.

3. **The best types of products to sell on eBay.**

   Everyone wants to sell the latest consumer product, but the truth is there is a lot of competition from established sellers and even big online companies that have discovered eBay. The best item to sell on eBay is something used or a very specialized niche product that few others are selling.

   Another great item is consumables. The idea here is to get repeat business via your website from customers who buy from you on eBay.

4. **Search listings on eBay to see what is selling.**

   Go to: http://listings.eBay.com to see what is listed and being sold on eBay. The number in parentheses after the category title is the number of auctions for a given item. In general, the higher the number, the more action and sales.

5. **Master niche marketing and specialize for success.**

This is home plate for your success strategy. Find your own niche. Define your market. Then you can know the type of person you're going to be selling to and the types of products you want to sell. You will also have less competition.

Forget trying to sell computers, digital cameras, Ipods, and plasma TVs. There is no way you can compete with the big guys unless you have tons of money. And those drop ship websites and programs that claim to have those products are mostly scams. Find a small niche, or several small niches that you can dominate.

Along with being in a superior position to take advantage of repeat business, the benefits of becoming specialized are endless. If you know more about your product area, you will be able to buy at better prices and people who sense you specialize in something will be more comfortable buying from you.

6. **Become an expert in your field.**

Become an authority on what you do in your online auction business. If you sell printer ink cartridges, you want to be thought of before anyone else.

When you become an authority in your field, a whole new universe of business and opportunity is opened up to you. I buy certain types of things on eBay from the same sellers over and over. I wouldn't dare do business with anyone else; not when they have proven themselves and their products.

You want to earn that same type of position in the minds of eBayer's for your niche. Also, continue your auction education. Read books and training manuals, visit the chat and message boards, attend an eBay University when it comes to your town, go to eBay Live, and keep learning all the time.

7. **Increase sales by putting audio in your auctions.**

I began using audio in my auctions in May 2004. I saw an immediate increase in sales.

I use a company called Seller's Voice for my audio. It's so easy. I just dial an 800 number, record my message, and then go to their website and copy a short line of code that I paste into my auction. If you launch your auction first, you can also record the message and just type the auction number into the phone and they will paste it in for you.

8. Get a sales tax number.

Contact the sales tax authority in your county or state offices to get a sales tax number. This will allow you to buy from many wholesale companies that would not deal with you otherwise.

If you're not sure who to contact in your state, just call your local chamber of commerce and they will advise you or give you the phone number or website address to register.

9. Your auction headline and description is where it all begins.

Your headline is your advertising and your item description is your salesperson. On the web, how your potential buyer perceives you and your product is everything.

Be sure to use power words in your auction title (headline). Rare, unique, powerful, new, unusual, stunning, top-notch, first-class, etc. Just be sure not to exaggerate. Don't call something rare if it's not.

Copywriting is the art of showing you and what you sell to the buyer in the best possible light. It's the most important thing you have going for you. A carefully crafted sales letter (item description) can increase your results exponentially without having to spend an extra penny.

10. Stand behind your product and service.

We offer an unconditional money-back guarantee on everything we sell. This has been our practice since our first day on eBay. Now if you're selling cars or houses or "as is" used goods, this may not be a good idea. But the simple offer of a satisfaction guarantee will dramatically increase your sales.

Even unhappy people rarely go to the trouble of sending something back. The cost of providing the few refunds will be far outweighed by the increased volume of sales. At the very least offer a guarantee your items are exactly as described ad you will give a full refund if they're not. If you have a return policy (and you should), be sure and spell it out clearly at the end of your auction description or in the form eBay gives you to do this.

For more helpful tips visit Skip at www.SkipMcGrath.com.

Amazon

Amazon was one of the first websites to have an online affiliate marketing program. Bloggers and website owners can make up to 15% in referral fees by promoting Amazon on their sites. There are several ways to link to Amazon by either creating text links, banners, aStores and widgets. You can add product image links and special Amazon promotion banners for a more unique display of Amazon content.

You can also easily create a whole online aStore to show multiple products and product details. With widgets, your customers can listen to samples of music and view slideshows of your favorite books. Amazon also provides you with tips on how to better use their marketing resources to drive traffic to your site and sell more products. You can check out the latest updates to the affiliate program on Amazon's associate blog.

Article Writing

If you're a good writer, writing articles is a great way to drive people to your site. And if you're not a good writer, hire a good writer to write them for you. Articles are free marketing. Any number of people could pick up your article and post it to their ezine, website or book.

These should be about topics that your readers would be interested in. Have a few of them that are about 500 to 700 words in length with killer headlines that will grab a reader's attention. Put them on your site to use as content. This will drive traffic to your site.

Use articles from others with their permission on your site. Include articles in your newsletter for your readers. Then archive them on your site.

Establish yourself as an expert through article writing. Pick a small niche and be a big fish in a small pond. People feel more comfortable buying from people that are experts and really know what they're talking about. Establish credibility with your audience.

At the bottom of the article you need to have a resource/ bio box that includes your name, website, and maybe even a freebie. This should be written in third person and shouldn't sound like an advertisement for your business.

If you are the expert, be bold in telling the readers what they need to do. Don't beat around the bush. If you're a landscape expert, tell them exactly how to dig up their bulbs and store them for the winter. Use action verbs to get your message across and really make it stand out. Motivate people to take action. Be precise and to the point.

Write articles in your own voice. People searching for information want to find something new that they didn't know about. Give them new and unique information and put it in your own unique voice.

Once you've composed some articles, get them to article distribution sites. Look them up by searching for "article directories". Once they're published, other sites and newsletters will also begin to publish them with your contact box, which contains your website info, and you will improve your positioning with the search engines.

Stress the benefits of whatever it is you are covering in your article. Tell people how to save money, improve their memory, live longer, sleep better, etc. Always tell them about the benefits.

Your article subject matter should only cover one topic. Don't try to cover everything all at once.

You know how I always stress "Be unique"? The same thing applies to your articles. Give people something they haven't seen before. Cover a topic from a different angle that no one else has covered. Write the article in an informal way that appeals to your readers. If you are using terms they aren't familiar with, explain them clearly. Tell personal stories in your articles that your readers will relate to and want to hear about. Let them know how *you* solved a problem.

Proofread your articles with and without your spell-checker. It won't pick up everything, so it's important to check it yourself.

Submit your articles to directories and also to newsgroups. Pick a few that relate to your topic and check them out for a while to see what kind of information they use. Then send them an email to tell them about your articles and ask if they would like to use them.

Contests & Giveaways

This is by far the best marketing tool I've found. I started by going to marathons and wearing swiggies in full view of the runners. Of course they would ask me what they were and I would say "If you'll wear them in the race, I'll give you a set".

Most people were thrilled to do it. They had a cool, new product to wear, plus they were really hydrated during the race. And it was great exposure for swiggies. This targeted the exact people that I wanted to target and it leveraged an existing social network, which was the runners. I never forced it on anyone. I just waited for the right people to approach me. I gave them something for free and they gave me exposure for my product. It's a win-win.

Later, I would sit and observe from a distance as one person showed them to another person, and then another. Then they would start looking for me, the swiggies chick, giving away cool free stuff. And I did this every single weekend. But, I finally realized that it was just too slow getting the word out, and I needed to increase the pace tenfold or more.

So, I started calling marathons to find out if they'd like free products for their goodie bags. Most of them were thrilled. The bigger marathons charge to put your products in their goodie bags, but not all do. So, I just kept calling until I found the ones who would use them and shipped them out.

You can and should try the same technique. Find your target audience and offer to donate your products. That will get your audience talking, and you'll find even *more* fans. Take your products to the people who will use them. Let's say you have a new fishing product. Go to fishing clubs, fishing organizations, and fishing blogs and websites. Offer to give them some of the product for free if they will use them as contest prizes and giveaways. I've gotten customers and distributors by having people call me who have seen others wearing them. So I know firsthand that this method gets results.

You can also have contests on your own website. Have some kind of silly promotion with a giveaway. (If it's wacky and unique enough it might also get you some PR.) I started getting contacted by a lot of mom blogs for the kids swiggies. Just as you can give away free stuff on your blogs from others, blogs are a very good way to go when it comes to giving away your own stuff. It's a win-win all the way around. The blog gets free stuff to give away and traffic to their site. You get exposure in your target market. And the customer gets free swag. Blogs can also get traffic to their own site just by mentioning your contest or the blogger's contest.

Another one of the oldest and most effective ways to get new customers is by giving away free samples. Once people try them and like them, you've got a customer for life. If you're confident and believe in your product, you should have no trouble conveying that to the people you give your samples to.

When I first came out with the all natural, sugar-free electrolyte drink mix, I was originally planning on only selling it to kids. But after giving out free samples at a 50K Ultra Trail Run to see what the hard-core runners thought of it, I realized it was going over with that crowd as well as kids. It was safe enough for kids, yet powerful enough for the athletes.

The more you actually get out and test your product or service, the more you learn about your customers and how to improve and expand your product line.

By the way, I got to work the races at the medical tent because of an EMT who was in charge. He let me promote my HydroSport drink mix by giving it away to the runners when they came in suffering from dehydration. He helped develop it because he's diabetic, and wanted something sugar-free and all natural to give to the runners to treat them. He uses it at all of his races now because he really believes in it. What started as a giveaway turned into a great way to network with another business for a win-win situation.

Contest Tips:

■ Contact other companies and ask them if they would like to donate prizes for your blogs, websites and events. Give them free advertising and links, and mention them in your event programs. You can also review them on your site. Buy some merchandise to give away. It's well worth the cost.

■ Go to forums and contest sites to post your contest. Make sure you have good prizes that appeal to your readers.

■ Have a contest at a trade show. This will drive people to your booth. Make it a high value prize and you will get lots of traffic. Not everyone will be a perfect customer for you, but having a bust booth creates buzz. People will stop at a high traffic booth just to see what the fuss is all about.

■ Post your contests on social networking sites. Advertise them wherever you can. Get other bloggers to post it on their sites and offer them extra entries if they do. When the contest is over, post the winners on your blog or website and send them their prizes, or have the manufacturer send them the prizes.

Newsletters

A newsletter is a printed report or letter that contains news of interest to a certain group. A free newsletter can help build rapport with your customers and help you maintain contact with them. It keeps your customers updated on what your business is doing and reminds them to buy more often.

People really do want to buy your products or services, but they get busy and forget. Stay on their minds with a well-timed newsletter. A newsletter should inform and entertain, but it should also do some selling and cross-selling. Introduce new products and services whenever you can.

Read and study a variety of newsletters from different industries to get a feel for how they look and how successful they are at getting and keeping your attention. You can send newsletters to customers or even to your distribution chain, like reps and distributors.

Include articles about your customers, and what distributors are doing to promote your products, especially if it helps others solve a problem. If a distributor gets a big sale, let everybody else know about it. Include a new use for one of your products. This will help other distributors in their sales efforts. Include special sales and closeouts.

The writing style should match your business and your own personal style. If you sell a humorous product, keep it light and funny. If it's a serious topic, keep the style of the newsletter serious. Include special offers that you could only find in the newsletter. Include coupon clippers with a percentage off or a free gift.

Newsletters can be very effective in certain businesses as long as they are permission based. This should be done by sign-ups, so you need to make it worth the recipient's while to read it. Put a form on your website. Make it obvious and easy to get to, like on the first page. It's best to use a double opt-in system where you send them an email requesting that they confirm the sign-up. That will eliminate any questions about spam. A good company to work with in developing a newsletter is Constant Contact. They will help you build your email list, email promotions, and will send out your email newsletters.

So, what should you put in your newsletter? A good email newsletter should contain eighty per cent information and twenty percent sales material. Email newsletters are much cheaper to produce than a printed version. And, use color. Studies have shown that readers are three times more likely to read your newsletter if you add a second color to it. Headlines and captions should also be done in color.

Some newsletters focus on one specific subject per issue and come under the heading of a theme newsletter. Try to put some kind of benefit in the tagline and make it timely. Why should the reader read it and why should they read it now?

You can either write your own articles for your newsletter or have someone else write them. You can also use a combination of both. Write about a subject that creates a need for your products or services. For example, a garden product manufacturer could write an article about the best time to plant certain vegetables.

Your articles should include industry information, product reviews, contests, interesting visuals, bullet points, calendars, quotes, how-to information, and other news of interest to your readers. Always make sure they have a reason to go to your website for more.

If you're stuck for something to write about, the best way to think of it is that you're trying to solve a problem for your readers. What problem did you have and what did you do to solve it? That's what your readers want to hear about.

You can copyright your newsletter by writing "Copyright" and the year and name of the person or company. But to register it for legal action you need to send it to the Copyright Office and register it through them. You can copyright the content, but not the name.

Give your readers a special offer. This could be a special report or free ebook. Create buzz by having contests and short surveys. If you sell several products, only include one in each newsletter. Then you should go into detail about that one product. Look for different angles for each product. Newsletters make your customers feel like they are involved in the progress of your company.

Use lots of headings, subheadings, and short chunks of text. Include order forms and other ways people can order your product. Try to keep your newsletter short. You'll have a better chance of getting it read. You should have a consistent look and feel to your newsletters. You want your readers to instantly recognize them. As soon as you finish one, start working on the next one.

Have a fixed schedule of when they get mailed out, and stick to it. Try to spread your communication out so they don't get too much at once. Try to mail out at least once a month. Be familiar enough with your industry to be able to time the mailings according to your industry cycles.

Anticipate that you might run out of things to say in your newsletter. This happened to me the first time and I just quit writing it. The next time I was a little more prepared and had information stored up in advance. Try to get as much stored up as possible.

Once your readership is pretty high, ask others to write guest articles in exchange for promotion for them. Or do an interview with them. Either way gives them more publicity and gets their name and website out there.

Like websites, you can also sell advertising in your news-letter. If you don't want to do it yourself, you can get an advertising broker to help you. Or, you can barter ads with other newsletters. Paid ads work well for non-profits, classifieds, and associations or clubs.

If you do sell ads in your newsletter, you'll need a rate card. Sometimes non-profits can find a sponsor to cover the costs of the whole newsletter. If you get your newsletter to a certain level you can charge ad rates at cost per thousand or cpm. You can also advertise your site in other people's email newsletters. Create your own ad for that business or for one of your other businesses and use it in the newsletter.

Tips for using newsletters:

■ You can send your newsletters via email, but another way is to create an HTML web page or blog just for the newsletter. You can then send out emails to let everyone know it's available.

- If you're a manufacturer, include a printed copy of your newsletter in the shipments you send out.
- From the first issue, ask your readers for feedback. That will help you figure out what they are really interested in and will steer you in a clearer direction.
- Events should include a calendar, date of event, directions, and RSVP information.
- You may eventually want to consider franchising your own newsletter to similar businesses. For example, there are lots of real estate newsletters which, for a fee, allow a realtor to put their own picture and name on the newsletter and send it out.
- Archive your newsletters on your website or get someone else to archive them for you. Then your readers can check out your past issues.
- Make sure your newsletter is in all of the newsletter search engines.
- Always make sure they can unsubscribe easily if they want. If your unsubscribe rate goes up, find out why.

Ezines

Ezines are just magazines that are online instead of in hard copy. They can be website based or email based. Some provide the whole version of their traditional magazine, some only publish limited articles, and some publish last month's edition.

Like direct mail, ezines are sent out to a very targeted audience. They're reading the ezine because they're interested in the subject matter.

There are thousands of ezines online. Find one that caters to your target market. You can advertise in them or submit articles to them with your website in the byline and a hyperlink if they'll allow it. You can also start your own ezine and get others to advertise in yours.

Don't choose an ezine just by the number of subscribers. Sometimes you can get a better response by narrowing down the niche, even if the number of subscribers is not as high. Before you start advertising, subscribe to the ezine and become familiar with it. Contact the advertisers and ask them if they are happy with the results they've gotten from the ezine. Track your responses to each newsletter by using different email accounts.

Word of Mouth

One of the best ways to grow your business is by word of mouth. You know, like the old Breck shampoo commercial "I told two friends and they told two friends . . ."

Word of mouth spreads from one person to the next without the help of advertising. What better way to get the word out about your business than to have a huge network of people singing your praises? Every time you make a sale and the customer is happy, that's one more chance to have another person recommending your product or service.

It works for big corporations and it works for small mom and pop stores, as long as you give people something to talk about.

According to the Technical Assistance Research Program for the U.S. Department of Consumer Affairs "it costs five times more to obtain a new customer than it does to retain an existing one". So, there's no better investment than keeping your customers happy, and that leads to more word of mouth.

If you want people to spread the word about your product or service, you need to have a great product. It also helps to have something that's unique. People like talking about something new and interesting. And they like to be the first to know about it. You can't be boring. This is why I always stress being unique. There is always a way to put a new and different twist on anything. Keep digging until you find it.

The first thing I ask my PR clients is "What's special, unique or different about you?" Many times I'm met with "Well . . . uh . . . uh . . ." Find a way to be special, unique or different.

Make someone's day. The more you make the customer feel good, the more they'll spread the word about your excellent customer service.

Look for your most enthusiastic customers. It could be the ones that spend the most money, or it could be the ones who genuinely love your products and recommend others to your site. Also, if someone takes the time to sign up for a newsletter or email list, you can bet they are true fans. Keep them happy and keep giving them something great to talk about.

There is a woman who calls me every time she sees swiggies in a magazine or on a TV show. Funny thing is, she's never ordered from me, but she always makes sure I know when my product is in the news. Sometimes people just like to be helpful.

I had T-shirts and tote bags made up with swiggies and HydroSport logos on them. I would offer to send them out free if distributors asked for them. I knew that the ones who asked would be out wearing them and promoting the brand name.

Your reps, distributors, and employees are also excellent sources of word of mouth promotion. I have reps who wear swiggies everywhere they go and even have magnetic signs that they put on their cars with the swiggies logo, etc. Then they put their own phone number on it to capture leads. Make it easy for them by supplying these tools for them to use.

It helps when your talkers are members of a club or association. That spreads the message even faster. I always make sure I give away swiggies to members of running clubs. They use the product and many others instantly see it.

Every month I make sure I donate as many swiggies as I can to charities who sponsor walk-a-thons and marathons. This is a win-win for both of us. The charities get free, unique swag, and I get people out using swiggies in marathons where everyone else will see them. They will also usually mention swiggies in their programs and newsletters. And for me, it's also a tax write-off.

I have a box full of cards and letters from customers who were happy with my products and services and took the time to write and tell me about it. Talk about making your day! I also do the same when I get good (and bad) customer service myself. I think the people at the top of an organization need to know how their business is being run. Word of mouth from bad service travels fast. When you're treated badly by a company, people tend to rant about it, so it's important to read all the feedback letters you get and make corrections quickly.

We buy from people and companies we trust. And when we have a good experience with a company, we'll tell our friends about it. And they'll tell their friends. Customer experiences will drive more word of mouth sales than a typical ad will, so treat your customers right and give them a good experience.

I have a handful of restaurants that I go to all the time. Their food and service is always consistently good, and they know me by name when I walk in. And I always recommend them to other people. That's worth more than any ad. How many times have you seen a great movie and rushed out to tell everyone you know about it? You can't pay for that kind of advertising.

Get your product in the hands of the trendsetters. Maybe that means a celebrity or maybe it's the people who others in a particular group admire or look up to. For example, I sold some swiggies to an ultra marathoner in Australia named Wayne "Blue Dog" Gregory. Wayne placed in an ultra marathon wearing swiggies for the last leg of the race. He had them frozen and used them to keep his body temperature down during the hottest part of the race. Anyone watching Blue Dog certainly saw the swiggies he was wearing. Since his peers look up to him, this was a big boost to the swiggies brand. And he gave me a great testimonial, which is another part of word of mouth marketing.

A great thing bloggers do is to have giveways and contests. I was already doing giveaways, so working with bloggers was just another extension of that. Customers who are actively encouraged to interact with your brand, as readers of a blog are, will likely tell others about it. For example, I could work with a running blog to hold a contest where users would send in their favorite pictures of themselves or others wearing swiggies. I would donate a prize as a reward for the winner. Then, the blog posts the pictures on their website.

How can *you* engage *your* customers? Be creative. User-created content can create indefinite buzz.

And, if you're using testimonials like me, an effective way to use them is to have them rotate on your site. Just show one testimonial and use an animated GIF file to rotate from it to many others. Testimonials added to other people's websites and marketing material also works to your advantage by showing you as the expert and getting your name out there.

Tips on using word of mouth:

- Make someone's day. The more you make the customer feel good, the more they'll spread the word about your excellent customer service.
- Make sure your word of mouth fans are given access to a special "club". Give them behind the scenes info, merchandise and other goodies that you don't make public. Thank them any way you can.
- If a customer complains and you go out of your way to fix the problem, you'll probably gain a loyal customer. People who don't complain when they get bad service will probably never buy from you again. So, feedback is good. Look at the complaint from the customer's point of view. Never take it personally. Look at customer complaints as a way to improve your business. People like to return favors when you do something nice for them.

If you fix the problem they have, they will usually buy from you again, and are more likely to tell others what a great company you are. Exceed your customer's expectations. Go the extra step to make them happy.

- Social networks like Facebook have lots of "friends" recommending things. Tap into these communities. Build a good reputation within a niche community. To get the word out about swiggies I contacted as many mom bloggers as I could find. They not only blog about them on their sites, but they also link to other blogs, and moms recommend products and services they like. This expands your network quickly.

- Have your website become "the authority" on a particular topic. A trusted expert who is there to answer questions, offer advice and give direction. Soon, people will be spreading the word that your site is *the* place to go. Have other authorities give you testimonials to use on your website and in your marketing materials.

- Get customers to give you testimonials. Some will just do it on their own, and you'll have to ask others if they'll give you one. Testimonials give credibility to your product. Make sure you get permission to use them. You can also use audio and video testimonials for added effect. Include their name and website address of the people giving testimonials for extra credibility. This helps both of you.

Networking

A network is a web of people that are connected directly or indirectly to the links of the people in the network. These could be friends, acquaintances, other business owners, members of a club, or your family.

People in a network trade contacts, referrals, and information. It's not done to get something in return. If it's done right and in the spirit of giving, don't worry, it will come back to you. The more you give to your network, the more you are depositing in the karma bank. Sometimes it can take years to reap a reward from one of your networks. It may come from another one or it may come in the form of a huge payoff from that network down the line.

The reason it takes so long to see benefits is because nobody is going to do you a big favor if they don't know you. How close are you to people you grew up with or went to college with? If you've just met someone and you don't really hang out with them or keep in contact with them, why would they jump through hoops to do you a favor?

A friend of mine set out to help other people and connect others in her writing network. Instead of asking for favors, she did favors for everyone else. And she stayed on everyone's mind. So, when the time finally came to hire a writer that fit her qualifications, her name was on everyone's mind in a favorable light. In the end, she got the dream job she wanted without ever asking for it.

Have multiple networks for different businesses. I have one network that was created because we were all conned by the same con artist. And believe me, it's a big network! I set out to find everyone this guy had conned, and in doing so met a lot of nice, hard working entrepreneurs. We've now connected and we all help each other. We were drawn together by a bad situation, but turned it into something good. A network can become stronger when everyone knows each other. Be aware of who the people are around you and the opportunities that could transpire because of knowing these people. Constantly brainstorm to think of ways you can help connect people. Sometimes it's not the most obvious way.

Sometimes I've found that it's easier to make a call for someone in my network than it is to make the call for myself. You're removed from the situation and it's less like you're asking for a favor.

You can also make requests from your network. Try asking for recommendations, ideas, and information before asking for a job. If they know what you do and you are right for something, they will ask you.

To get an idea of how powerful a network is, try to picture how many people each person in your network knows. Then think about how many different networks you have yourself. The whole six degrees of separation starts to make sense. You never know who someone is or who they know. Don't assume that because they're parking your car or cleaning your house that they don't have valuable people in their network. These have been some of my best networking connections.

Hairdressers know everyone and they also know everyone's secrets. They make great matchmakers. My own hairdresser has made a lot of money as a middleman just by knowing people and matching them up. (Taking a cut, of course.) The receptionist at a movie studio can be the head of the studio tomorrow. Always treat everyone with respect and you can't go wrong.

One benefit of having a network is that you get to learn from their mistakes. With the con artist's network I was able to figure out his M.O. and how the victims before me solved their problems. In turn, I have been able to save others from the same fate. People like saving others from making mistakes. That's one reason I wrote this book.

Being an entrepreneur can be a lonely business. But when you have a network of other entrepreneurs who are going through the same problems, it makes it easier to handle and more fun in the process.

"Serendipity" is when you accidentally discover something good, especially when you're looking for something else. Just like you increase your odds of winning the lottery when you buy multiple tickets, you increase your odds of serendipity when you have one or more networks. I have a saying that I posted next to my computer . . . "If you want to be in the right place at the right time, you have to be everywhere all the time." It just means you need to get out there as much as possible to as many places as possible that relate to your business. Eventually, something good will happen.

Sit down and make a list of all the people in each of your networks. You'll discover that you have many more than you realize. Now, how many of those do you keep in touch with on a consistent basis? Start right now. Give them a quick call or email and then keep it up. I'm constantly having to remind myself to keep in touch. People have lives. They get busy. Put a note over your computer if you have to to remind you.

Discover your common interests. Organize events with others in your network who have similar interests. I've always liked mixing business with pleasure. I like bowling, and I'm going to go bowling anyway. I might as well bowl with people that are in my network that I like hanging out with anyway. It's a great way to have fun and get some non-formal business done.

Just like you have your old friends and new friends, the same is true for networking contacts. Have your list and constantly add on to it. The best way to do this is to get out and meet people at industry functions. Join your local Chamber of Commerce, Toastmasters, and other business organizations. One of the best ones I've found is Count Me In, an organization for women business owners. After attending just one event, I ended up with a bank loan, two big swiggies orders, and two round-trip plane tickets. That was without doing any networking at all.

Being a part of a club or organization will put you in contact with others who share your interests and are at different levels in your business. Sometimes you help others, sometimes others help you.

Bring your business cards and other marketing material and be prepared to hand them out. Get out of your shell and go up to people and introduce yourself. It won't kill you. Get used to doing it. Be friendly and smile. Remember people's names and use them often. Be the matchmaker and introduce someone you know to someone they need to know.

Include others in the conversation and really hone your listening skills. Ask questions about their business and what they are doing now, and what they'd like to be doing. Maybe you can help them. Be interested in them and be interesting yourself. Have a few topics of conversation ready to talk about.

Meet as many people as you can, and get as many business cards as you can from relevant contacts. When you get home, put them in some kind of order. Send out cards within a few days while it's still fresh in your mind and theirs. Make notes on the business cards about what you talked about and anything you need to remember about the person.

One of the best ways to network is to volunteer for the club or association you are a member of. Not only will you be privy to the inside information, but, you'll get to know everyone on a more intimate level. Especially volunteer to be a liaison between the guest speakers and the group. This gives you more of a chance to get to know them personally. It also helps you hone your leadership abilities.

Get involved in community events. This could be a parent's group, book club, church group, sports club, or even just a neighborhood block party. Anywhere that you can get out and meet people and expand your network. A great place to network is a wedding, birthday party, or holiday party.

One of the easiest things to ask for and the easiest thing to get is referrals. People like to refer good contacts, and word of mouth is the best form of advertising.

MORE NETWORKING TIPS:

- A network is something that needs constant work. You keep adding to it, while maintaining the contacts you already have.
- You should think of the people in your network as friends. Hang out with them. Take them to lunch. Send

them Christmas cards. Keep them up to date on what you're doing and ask them to do the same with you. You never know when someone in your other networks can help a new or old contact.

- Use your skills to help others. One of my most valuable skills is PR. I always try to help others by using that skill when I can, and the people I help are more than happy to send me a testimonial.

- Thank the people in your network on a constant basis. People never get tired of hearing it and most people don't say thank you enough. A hand-written thank you card goes a long way.

- Get used to starting conversations with people. It doesn't come naturally for me, but I try to talk to people wherever I can. Unless you get the look that says "get out of my space", try to say something nice to someone and make small talk.

- Make a habit of remembering people's names. I'm really bad about this, so I try to make a conscious decision to remember. And if you don't, it's okay to ask them to tell you again. People love to be called by their name.

- Make sure everyone has a way to reach you and always include your signature line with your emails.

- Be the person that everyone comes to for information. It's a good way for people to stay in touch with you, and they will remember you as someone who does good for others.

- Use different methods for following up. Make phone calls, send emails, and send postcards and letters. Have a box of thank you cards and send one whenever someone does something nice for you. Always make them personal by hand writing them, and also by mentioning something you have talked about.

■ Have a customer appreciation party for your best customers. If that's too overwhelming, at least take some of them out for lunch occasionally.

Co-founder of the Flash Forward Institute, Suzanne Lyons, came up with a unique networking seminar that stresses the value of relationships in networking as being the key to success in every business:

Early on in my producing career here in Los Angeles, I would be at a party or event, and all too often people would approach me and say "Suzanne, I hear you're a film producer. I'm an actor. Here's my headshot." Or "Hi, my friend told me you're a producer. I'm a director. Here's my reel." It drove me crazy! In every other business in the world we create relationships (or should) first. Don't just jump right into action, create a relationship first. Talk about the possibility of working together, the opportunity and the benefits it could provide, and then and only then, make a request.

It was because of this that I created a seminar called "The Magic and Power of Career Relationships". Because in the entertainment industry, like every industry, networking is critical, and yet, most people have absolutely no idea how to do it or do it properly. The goal is to create authentic relationships.

So, in the workshop, every week for the six weeks of the program, the homework was to have a party. And at the party you were not allowed to talk about your career. So often when we are meeting people for the first time, or when we are in a group of people, we get nervous and feel comfortable only talking about our jobs and careers.

The idea of not being allowed to talk about your career for six weeks really helped people break that habit. So, if you like hiking you would invite your friends to go hiking, and you would ask them to bring along the casting director friend of theirs, because you've done your homework and know she likes hiking as well. Or you know that director you've wanted to meet likes gourmet cooking as much as you do, so you ask a friend of yours who knows him to invite him to your gourmet food cooking party. Your friends feel comfortable inviting their friends because they know you're not going to talk about anything other than hiking or gourmet cooking.

What surprised me was that during the six week seminar the participants got more jobs than in any of the Flash Forward seminars combined!

Here are eight tips on networking and creating relationships that can help you break the ice and break through your fear:

1   Take full responsibility for creating relationships. Put out your hand and say "hi". At a party make a point of meeting at least two people and don't leave until you've accomplished that goal. Don't just exchange business cards, really get to know them.

2   If there is something that you really admire, begin with an authentic acknowledgement. This is something that is missing in our culture. It will make them feel great and will put you at ease since the emphasis will be on them and not you.

3   Another way to create relationships is by using referrals. If you know someone who knows someone you want to meet, have them make the introduction or at least ask if you can use their name when you call to set up a meeting.

4   Try to set up meetings with people. We tend to get lazy today and use email too often. Get face-to-face with people as much as possible, or at least talk to them on the phone. Make it easy for people to say yes. One way to do this is to say "I'd love to have ten minutes of your time". Everyone can fit in a ten minute meeting. Make a list of people you want to meet and give yourself a timeline to do it in.

5   Write down four or five interesting, unusual, unique, wonderful, remarkable, memorable things about yourself that have nothing to do with your career. You always want to be remembered and this is a great way to ensure that.

6   When possible, do some research on the person you're going to be meeting. Know who they are and learn about their company. It will impress them and make a difference. It's another way to put them at ease since you're talking about them.

7   Another way to create relationships with people on your list that you really want to meet is to volunteer to produce and lead a panel. It's a great way to get to know them on a one-on-one basis.

8   Have fun! Be yourself! If you're nervous, say so. Make light of it. There are over 5 billion of us on the planet. It's just one big giant sandbox and we're here to play together and have fun. So stick your hand out and say "hi".

Suzanne Lyons is an award-winning film producer and seminar leader. She is co-founder of Snowfall Films, Inc., Windchill Films, Inc., and the Flash Forward Institute. Suzanne teaches workshops on filmmaking and has published an ebook on How to Produce Your Film.

PROMOTIONAL MARKETING

A promotional product is any kind of product that is branded with a logo to promote the company that is giving it away.

Nearly everyone's been given some kind of promotional product, whether it's a pen, hat, t-shirt, or mug with a company's logo on it. In fact, if you look around, you probably have several of them. I decided to see how many promotional items I had lying around. I found an MP3 player, a spatula, a piggy bank, a hat, a bottle opener, several shirts, a teddy bear, a calculator, a jacket, and many pens and pencils. These were all products that were given to me by corporations just so I would remember their brand. I could tell you which corporation gave them to me, even though some of them are several years old. Studies have shown that most people tend to remember the company's name that they saw on a promotional item.

Promotional products aren't just pens and t-shirts. Today, there are thousands of items in the promotional market that are used to thank customers, draw in visitors at trade shows, generate sales leads or introduce new products. Companies use promotional products when they are opening a new business or promoting an event.

Promotional products have a value that's more than the cost of the item. People love free stuff and if you give them something they will use, they'll tend to keep it.

A promotional product can provide constant reinforcement of your brand name. And if the item is something they wear, they'll be walking advertisements for your brand. A quality product also creates a favorable impression of your company.

Offer free promotional products with your logo on them to your best word of mouth talkers. You can find them by going to the Advertising Specialty Institute (ASI) or any number of promotional product companies. Make sure you include your company's website on the promotional item. Find a unique and useful promotional item that fits with your business and will remind people of your company whenever they use it.

I sell a lot of swiggies in the medical and insurance industries. It's a healthy, unique, and useful product for people to stay hydrated. The company's logo gets noticed, and people will remember the product and where it came from.

A great example of a useful promotional item is the calendar. My realtor sends me a small magnetic calendar that stays on my refrigerator year-round. It has her picture and all of her contact information on it, and so I always know how to reach her.

You can tie an item into the theme of an event. Or, if you have a service business, promotional items may be used to remind customers that they should make an appointment to see you.

Use free promotional products as a "call to action". For example, if you are selling something and want the customer to buy, then offer them a free gift. This free gift can be a promotional product with your logo on it.

Barry O' Dwyer of Brand Reminders.com, a promotional products company in the U.K., gives small business owners advice about using promotional products to grow their business:

Why should small business owners use promotional products?

Given the chance, any small business owner would like to look into the face of a potential customer, shake their hand, and from that moment they have an opportunity to "bond" with that person and explain what they have to offer. That situation however is for most of us not possible. Sending out a promotional product sample or giveaway does the next best thing because, like the handshake, it's tactile with two additional benefits. The first is that the item can be of practical use, and secondly, it can carry a message. This leads me to the following point.

How does a company know what type of promotional product to buy?

It's always nice to be creative and give something new. However, to my mind, even more important is to make the item relevant to the targeted audience and to the marketing objective in mind. The big mistake that so many companies make is to personalize the latest "hot product" without giving careful consideration to those who are going to receive it. (Do you really need another pen?) Brand Reminders was recently asked by a major U.K. TV production company to come up with a giveaway for promoting a new TV series. The venue was a trade festival in a hot climate. We proposed that the series title/logo and website was printed on tubes of sun cream and tubes of after sun. This was felt to tick all the right boxes and both products were freely distributed amongst selected delegates. Every time the products were used, the TV series was noticed again and again with the added benefit that the user didn't get sunburned—a win-win situation all around.

Do you help the business owner put together a campaign or do they have their own ideas?

Sometimes the owner has very strong ideas on what they want, and if they wish to proceed with their idea, that's fine by me. I will source the product and ask a few relevant questions to see if the supplier has a track record. I'll ask whoever else has purchased the product, obtain a sample, and if all is okay, arrange to present the customer with a visual showing the logo or message prior to production. However, if I can present a better solution I will. This can only be done if I have the opportunity of working directly with the end user and get to understand what the objective of the promotion is. On a lot of occasions the client's promotions company tell me what's required and I just source the product and have it produced. This can be problematic in that I firmly believe in having an interest in what I'm doing. Luckily they leave that to the experts!

How can a company tell if their promotional advertising campaign was successful?

This depends on what you call successful. Were you trying to obtain a set number of sales leads? Or driving your audience to visit your website? Whatever the objective, was the idea involved tested? Was the promotional item researched to test the reaction amongst those about to receive it? What about the all-important headline that will decide if the text gets read? How did that grab the readers? Was it compelling? The answer is, prior to running out the full campaign, many of the component parts should have been tested. How else will you know if it's to be successful? The bottom line is to write down clear objectives and know who you want to target and what you want to accomplish.

AFFILIATE MARKETING

Affiliate marketing is where online merchants pay website owners on a performance only basis to promote their products or services. It works a little like a finder's fee. It's a win-win for the merchant and the website owner. The merchant gets his product on many sites without paying for advertising and the website owner makes money by just placing an ad on his site and collecting money. The amount of commission should be enough for it to be worth it for the website owner, and the merchant needs to really know who they're working with so they make sure they get paid. Affiliate marketing is like having a big sales force out working for you that you only pay if they make a sale.

When I first started out with swiggies, I didn't really know that much about affiliate marketing, but I just used common sense and figured that if a site is already selling fitness products, maybe they could sell mine too, and their customers would get a discount. It took years to get the affiliates, but once I did, it just kept going. I still have most of the same affiliates today. It's quite time consuming to do it that way, but when you don't have enough money to join a big affiliate network, it's worth the time and energy.

The most common form of affiliate program is the per sale program. If an affiliate send you a customer who buys something, the affiliate gets paid a percentage or a flat fee. Commissions usually pay anywhere from 1–15%. Amazon. com pays up to 15% commission on sales, but like most merchants, they have a sliding scale fee payment.

A per inquiry affiliate program is when an affiliate gets paid when someone requests information. The merchant is hoping to turn those inquires into sales.

There are also pay per click programs. These have the most potential for fraud. When a click is registered, the cash register rings. You never know who's doing the clicking or if they're even real customers.

Two-tier programs are similar to multi-level marketing organizations like Amway. You receive a commission on what you sell *and* the affiliate sites that you recommend sell. Before getting involved with a program, figure out if it fits with what your website is selling.

Create the best banner ads you can that will stand out on an affiliate's site. Do everything you can to make it easy for your affiliates to promote it, and make sure you pay on time.

One benefit of having your own affiliate program is that it increases your search engine ranking. If you don't want to do it all yourself you can pay an affiliate program service to do it for you.

Once you get your affiliate software and your shopping cart up and running, you will still need to drive traffic to your site. Your website is still just a sign in the desert unless you actively promote it. Include your affiliate program in your overall marketing plan for the best results.

PUBLICITY

This is my favorite way to get the word out. Maybe I'm biased because I'm a publicist. But I think it's also one of the best and most cost effective ways to get your message out there.

Public relations is a strategy that a company develops for dealing with the media. This includes media exposure for a product, service, or event, or it could include damage control when bad press comes out.

Publicity builds up your brand name and lets everyone know who you are and why they should know you. People will tune out advertising and don't really trust it, but publicity is like a personal recommendation. Whose opinion would you trust, an announcer on a commercial, or your favorite TV host or newspaper writer who raves about a new product?

People are also easily bored and you have to get their attention. That's one reason anything unique and different gets the media's attention. Strive to create unique products, services, and events with a unique or unusual angle. Distinguish yourself from everyone else in your industry. You don't have to spend a lot of money to get the media's attention, you just have to have a great or unusual idea. Be your most unique self and wear it with confidence. That will attract the media to you. If you don't believe in yourself and your product, the public won't believe in it.

I did everything I could to make swiggies the best and safest product possible, so when I go on a show to promote it I really believe in them, use them myself, and believe they will work to help kids and adults stay cool and hydrated.

I think of publicity as "giving to get". Give the journalist or reporter what they want to get their story out there and make sure they make their deadline, and you'll get the exposure you want. Publicity should never be thought of as free advertising. Give them real news that is of value to their audience. Give them more than they expect. Be their researcher and supply them with statistics and sources.

I was asked to fly to New York to do a show once, but I couldn't make it. I spent the whole day calling everyone I knew who was an inventor with a new product that could do the show. I must have made a hundred calls and never found anyone. But I think the booker was pleased that I tried that hard. Help them do their job, and they'll think of you first when future opportunities arise.

I always keep files of other inventors and people in similar businesses so I can either recommend them if I can't make an interview or put together a panel of people if a producer asks. Keep information about others on file, and ask them to keep information about you on file. You never know when you might be able to help each other. I've gotten many people on local and national news shows with this approach.

Once, when a segment on a national news show had three inventors scheduled to show up, two of them couldn't fly there because of a blizzard. They called and asked if I knew any inventors who lived close by who could drive to the station to do the piece. Because I keep a file on hand, I was able to substitute two people at the last minute.

Helping producers out not only makes you look good, but it makes you feel good to be able to help out a fellow entrepreneur. It will come back to you. I promise.

Establish yourself as an expert and let everyone know what you do, especially the media. Get your message out on a regular basis. Let the media know that your organization is on the move.

Business newspapers may be especially receptive to your press release since they have smaller circulations. High school and college newspapers are another area to look into if you have a press release that would be of interest to their readers.

Don't start with the big national TV shows. Start locally with radio shows and local TV news shows. Get your feet wet first.

I once drove halfway across the country and stopped in every city along the way to do the news. I only got bumped off once because of a hurricane. (It was a little bigger news story than swiggies.) I had no idea what I was doing, but I just got on the phone in one city and started calling the next city to see if they could put me on the news. Then I'd drive until late at night, get a few hours of sleep, and get up at three or four in the morning to do a news show. I did so many shows, I could actually do the interviews in my sleep. (And I think some of them were!)

I was mainly working on small, local market news shows, but sometimes you get lucky. I pulled into New Orleans (a pretty big market) on a slow news day, and a local news crew took me out all afternoon to shoot around the French Quarter. We got very creative and I have a great tape of it.

Doing as many interviews as you can will help prepare you. I would take just about anything to get the practice. And you should too. If you're not used to being in front of the camera, an improv class may help you loosen up and be better able to think on your feet.

Work some stories, anecdotes, or statistics into your interview to keep it interesting. Don't oversell your product or service. Give out information on your topic and be helpful to the audience.

Even if you're prepared and well-seasoned, a reporter can always catch you off guard. They always seem to ask you one question you hadn't thought of. Don't get caught like a deer in the headlights. Know your information inside and out. I've noticed that most tend to have at least one devil's advocate question and usually more. Be prepared for them. They may pick up on an angle that you aren't pushing or hadn't thought of. Just run with it and make the best of it instead of trying to steer the interview in a different direction. Have backup pitches if they don't like the first angle. Make several suggestions and help them come up with an even better angle. But if they flat out say no, then thank them and move on to the next journalist or producer.

Media people move around a lot, so if you get a "no" from one reporter, give it some time and you could possibly pitch to the next person that takes their place. Make sure you rework your pitch the next time.

I did an interview for a national women's magazine, and they wanted to shoot a picture for the article. I suggested a local park and found a cool slide to use in the shot. It turned out great and they were happy with it. Use your creativity to help them, because by making their job easier you wind up with a more favorable piece and build a stronger relationship for the future.

Send them thank you cards after the interview. Keep in touch with them and let them know what you're doing. Ask them how they'd like to be contacted and put that info in your database.

Once you get started with the smaller media outlets, put together a press kit of all your clippings, and put your TV appearances on a CD. The more press you do, the more you become known as an expert in that field. They want to know that you can handle the interview, and having a press kit to send that shows successful print and TV interviews you've *already* done helps convince media people to work with you.

You can also put your appearances on video and show it at your trade show booth. This helps give you credibility and draws people to your booth. Always look for the pressroom during the show set-up. Drop off some press packets and keep some at your booth.

Think of ways to link your products, services, and events to what's happening in the news at the time. With swiggies and the electrolyte mix, I've sent out press releases during a heat wave and included a recent news article about it. I made sure to say that swiggies can be frozen to keep your body temperature down.

Make a list of the media you want to target. Make sure you do your homework and find out exactly what they want. Know a little bit about the magazines, newspapers, and TV shows you plan to pitch to. Buy copies of the magazines and actually watch the shows to see what kind of guests and topics they like.

Be sure to send press kits to the right person. And don't misspell their name. Never send the same release to more than one person at each newspaper. Update your media list regularly. People move around a lot.

Press releases should contain who, what, where, and why. They shouldn't be longer than a page in length, should be written in the style of a press release, and contain all of your contact information at the top and bottom of the page. Put a catchy headline at the top that gets their attention. A press kit can contain your press release, biography, show appearances, magazine articles, and your picture. Don't overload it with too much. If they want more information, they'll ask for it. You can also send a list of suggested questions to TV and radio producers, but not to journalists.

Giving producers a list of questions helps you as well as them. By the time you do your interview you should know everything about your product or service. By giving them the questions, you can be sure you know what they'll ask.

If you're promoting a product, make sure you have good quality pictures to send them. Having more than one shot for them to choose from is even better. Send your media contact an email to let them know that you've sent your press kit to them.

If you're putting on an event, get your press kit out at least six weeks in advance. Get it listed in the calendar sections of newspapers.

Make sure you keep up with which shows are on and off the air. I made the mistake of pitching to a show that had just gone off the air. Now I always have two TVs on at the same time and I channel-switch constantly. Make sure the show is still on before you talk to them. The same with magazines and newspapers. Also, make sure the people you want to pitch to are still there.

With a service based business, you might want to start establishing yourself as an expert in your field. Write articles for your trade's magazines. Write a letter to your local radio, TV, and newspapers and let them know you're available to give them information or quotes on a subject if they need it.

Send them clippings of other articles that quote you as an expert. Call them back in a week or so, but never right before their deadline.

Anne Leedom of Net Connect Publicity (an online PR firm) talks about how to choose an online publicist:

1. If it sounds too good to be true . . . it is. Beware of any company who makes extreme claims. We often help with damage control when clients have been taken in by the most abused claim heard today . . ."we can submit your site to 100 sites or more". Simply put, there are not that many credible websites on which to place your content. This is a red flag. A credible online publicist knows that real success comes in working with the best 10–20 sites and making those placements count.
2. Don't confuse an online publicist with a traditional publicist. An online publicist has dozens of relationships with websites who rely on them for experts. Results come from online publicists who know how to present to this medium and how to maximize the promotional support the site can offer in a timely way.
3. Avoid anyone who offers a "quick slam" campaign. You can't possibly receive any real value from placing one or two articles on any site, regardless of their size. Credible online campaigns work when appropriate websites are targeted, and submissions result in lasting relationships that continue for an extended period of time.
4. Choose an online publicist based on their contacts and experience. A credible online publicist has active relationships with editors of the sites on which you want to place your content.
5. Choose a publicist who knows how to secure fast and prominent placement. There are unique and rigid factors that are presented to an online editor in order to get prominent exposure on your targeted websites. Only work with a publicist who knows this process well.
6. Find a publicist that guarantees their placements. Credible publicists can and do guarantee their placements.
7. Work with a publicist who will take your entire campaign into consideration. An experienced online publicist will know everything necessary to secure prominent online positions for you, including how to assess your website, how to increase your search engine rankings, and how to format your content.
8. Choose an online publicist who provides stringent follow up. Once you've paid for your content to be submitted, it's crucial to make sure it got there and got to the right person.

9. Credible publicists create partnerships between you and online editors. Your publicist should be creating a variety of content features and opportunities for you. They can match what you have to offer with the needs of the sites, creating new and original features for the site that you will fill.
10. Avoid the cookie-cutter approach. A reputable publicist will customize their campaign objectives and their fees to your individual needs.

PUBLIC SPEAKING

According to Wikipedia, public speaking is "the process of speaking to a group of people in a structured, deliberate manner intended to inform, influence, or entertain the listeners.

The purpose can range from simply transmitting information, to motivating people to act, to simply telling a story."

Public speaking has come a long way since its beginnings in ancient Greece. Societies and cultures have changed, but the basic principles have remained the same.

Most people have some fear of public speaking, but if you're going to be a successful entrepreneur you need to get over it. There are too many opportunities to market your business that require you to speak in front of a group of people.

Your audience won't expect perfection, but they will expect to get something of value from your speech. That could be knowledge they didn't have before, a kick in the pants to get them started, or simply entertaining them and making them feel good about life in general. But give them something.

Don't waste their time.

How to give a great speech:

- Enjoy yourself and speak with passion about your topic and people will listen. Giving a good speech can motivate and inspire people to take action.
- Be yourself in front of your audience. Share some of your own weaknesses and the mistakes you've made. Be humble. People will relate to you if you're willing to open up and let them know who you are.
- Prepare cards, but don't read them. Just highlight your topics and glance at them if you need to. Number your cards in case you drop them.
- Even though you know your topic, make sure you do enough research to back up your arguments with evidence and learn a few statistics to throw in.

- Speak in a conversational tone and make a connection with your audience. Find some friendly faces in the crowd and make eye contact.
- Start off with a strong opening, sprinkle in some humor, some metaphors, and a few stories, then end your speech with a strong, positive close.
- Use humor in your speaking. Why? Because it works. It disarms the audience and makes you more likeable. Not only that, but it puts people in a better mood. And you want your audience in a good mood.
- Interact with your audience whenever possible. Solicit volunteers and carry out exercises.

■ Interweave some Powerpoints, flip charts, and props. Make sure you're comfortable with them. Just have them to show, and adlib from them.

By now you should be an expert on your topic. For example, if you've been a gardener and you know most everything there is to know about gardening, if you had to speak to a group of people about gardening, you would probably be confident enough about your knowledge to do it. Trust that you know your subject, and give that knowledge to others.

You don't have to be perfect, and the audience wants you to succeed because they want to learn from you. Practice makes perfect, so get out and speak as much as you can. You'll start out speaking for free to places like the Chamber of Commerce, Elks Club, Rotary Club, non-profits, churches, and schools.

Get out and network with anyone who could hire you or ask you to speak for free at their organization. Public speaking is a big referral based business. Make sure you bring plenty of business cards.

Offer to speak for free in exchange for other things, such as access to their mailing list, ability to sell your own books, or a promise to be able to speak in front of the key decision makers who could hire you in the future.

You can use your public speaking to get the word out about your company or brand and/or you can make money just from the speaking. You can either get paid directly by a company or you can get them to sponsor you as a speaker.

Veteran public speaker Ric Morgan shares some of his advice about public speaking:

■ The person who starts the business is the expert. Set yourself up as the expert.

■ Use your public speaking as a way of branding yourself and your business.

■ Don't make the speaking engagement a commercial for yourself.

■ Create a 30 minute presentation.

■ Tell them what you're going to say, say it, then tell them what you said.

■ Keep your presentation to 3 topics.

■ Have something the audience wants to hear.

■ Speak as often as you can—you can't learn how to speak by just reading a book.

Ric can be found at TheKeyNoteSpeaker.net

PUT IT INTO ACTION

☐ Make a list of local flea markets and trade shows
☐ Design a postcard for your product or service
☐ Start a website
☐ Create a blog for your business
☐ Make a list of everyone in your network
☐ Look into mailing lists in your target market
☐ Start a newsletter
☐ Brainstorm unique contest ideas
☐ Look for ezines that fit your target market
☐ Write a press release for your product (or hire someone to do it)

CHAPTER

6

Hiring Farmhands

"I get by with a little help from my friends."
—John Lennon & Paul McCartney

Even though you'll probably start your Money Garden on your own and work every job yourself until your business takes off, you'll eventually need help. It may not necessarily mean hiring employees right away, but if you're ever going to expand your business you'll have to get some help. In the beginning I think it's a good idea to do it all. That way you get to learn your business from the ground up in every department and you'll be in a better position of leadership once you do start hiring people. By then you'll know what works and what doesn't work.

The first people you'll want to turn to are family and friends. They want you to succeed and will probably be willing to help you out for some free pizza and beer. Years ago, when I was making swiggies in the U.S., I had to buy the parts separately and assemble them in my living room. I had a deadline to meet and no money to actually hire people to

187

put these together. So I had a pizza party and rented a movie. It was just mindless work that didn't need any real concentration, and the people who came were happy to help me out.

You can also almost always find college students who need some part-time minimum wage work. And if you have a non-profit, people are always willing to volunteer for a good cause.

DISTRIBUTORS & REPS

Since you can't be everywhere, you will eventually need a sales team, which will include distributors and representatives. Distributors are independent companies that buy the product from you and sell it to the end user. A manufacturer's rep also sells the product to the end user, but unlike the distributor, they don't warehouse the product. They sell and take a commission.

The job of a rep is to sell products to wholesale and retail buyers. They demonstrate the products and take orders. A rep can represent one manufacturer or several, and sell one product or a whole line of products. They may attend trade shows to network or find other products to represent. Sales reps can cover far more ground than you can on your own. They also usually have existing relationships with buyers that would take a long time for you to establish on your own.

Distributors buy inventory and store it in their warehouses. They can have hundreds or thousands of customers, which is good for you because it can open up new markets. The downside of that is your product getting lost in the process. The products that make the most money for them get the most attention. The upside is that you are selling volume. The distributor, like the rep, does all the work to get the product out.

Sometimes reps and distributors work together. The rep will get the sale and the distributor will ship the product out. Then the rep doesn't have to keep inventory in a warehouse.

I use both to sell swiggies. I have distributors around the world, and distributors *and* reps in the U.S. Both have their own independent businesses, but I work closely with them all to give them marketing and PR support.

Michael Rothschild of REDelicious in Australia gives us a point of view as an international distributor:

How is a distributor different from a rep?

As far as selling is concerned, both a distributor and a rep, even though they usually don't manufacture a product, need to act like the owner of that product. The customer of a distributor/representative does not differentiate between the owner of the company marketing the product and the company selling them the product. A rep must be equipped with all vital information pertaining to a product, and have the necessary sales techniques to convince a customer they need to buy their product. Excellent support from a rep's head office is also vital to success. The representative is the face of the company, the distributor is the body. Both must work efficiently.

A distributor needs to have the right selling techniques, but if they are importing their products, they must understand all government regulations in the country they are importing from, and also their own country. A distributor needs to have knowledge of currency exchange rates, freight costs, import duty, charges, and warehousing costs. These costs are seemingly innocuous, but can be the difference between profit and loss when their product is finally on a customer's shelf.

How do you work with reps?

It's important that reps feel a sense of ownership in our company. This does not particularly mean an actual equity stake, but keeping people in the loop on what we're doing in the company, new products that we're working on, updates, etc. Reps need to have an answer for every question a customer may ask, and therefore communication is, as with a good marriage, the number one point in having a sales force that generates maximum efficiency.

As an international distributor, do you have reps in other countries?

We have made contact with companies in countries such as France, Russia, Singapore, and China. We find it makes more sense to use contacts that are sometimes not even in the same product field as us, to help us find the right rep in a particular country.

These contacts have the local knowledge that can short circuit months or even years looking for a rep. Each country has its own laws and regulations and this knowledge is vital.

What should manufacturers know about selling their products in other countries?

As Australians, we have become used to the fact that if we wanted to be involved in a bigger slice of the pie, we must think globally. Australia has a population of just over 20 million people, within a world of 6.5 billion. So this export mentality is forced on us. Manufacturers, even in an economy such as the U.S. need to realize that the market is not just on their doorstep, but any person that can be reached by Internet, email, or phone is a potential customer. Manufacturers need to pinpoint the strengths of their products and research other country's needs and customs to see if their product suits that country. Once this has been done, import and custom laws need to be accessed, or I suggest finding a good contact in that country that can help with the import and distribution process. A good way is to make contact with local government agencies that can give a list of suitable companies that can help with this process. The world is global, but local knowledge cannot be under-valued.

REDelicious Imports is committed to introducing unique, environmentally friendly products to Australia and beyond.

Roger Wilson of Manufacturers Representative Profile (MRP) explains the relationship between manufacturers and reps:

How do most manufacturers find reps?

Most manufacturers rely on word of mouth. In fact, before we developed the MRP service, we used the same method, but eventually found that it wasn't reliable enough. Less than 25% of the agencies we selected were successful, which we later found to be the industry average. Three quarters of the agents were not successful and had to be replaced. We did a study to identify the factors that contribute to this problem and here are some of our findings:

The industry is over-populated in lines. A rep concentrates a major portion (usually 80%) of their sales efforts on 20% of their line package. The balance of their lines receive varying degrees of attention, but not their full sales effort.

There are over 200 types of accounts (classes of trade) an agent can sell or service in our industry, yet we found the average agency is usually efficient in selling and servicing 8 to 10 classes of trade. The combinations of these classes covered best, of course, vary greatly from one agency to another.

What is it so hard to find an appropriate rep to sell your line?

If you study their line, you have no way of identifying if those lines are comparable to your lines, and if they fall in the 80% or 20% category. You never know if they're going to push your product or not.

When the agent fills out information on the MRP and submits it to us, they have to make over 250 choices. We can identify the classes of trade which get their everyday selling attention, the lines they sell every day, match line compatibility, judge the strength of their management, and more.

Can a manufacturer sell direct to the retailer?

They could, but the rep has ongoing relationships with the retailers and understand their needs. Besides, reps also provide services like going into stores to make sure displays are showcased right, and that there is plenty of stock. They're in the stores constantly, something the manufacturer can't do.

What is the standard rep fee?

In the gift market a standard fee would be 15%. In wholesale or chain stores it could be around 10%.

VIRTUAL ASSISTANTS

According to the International Virtual Assistants Association, a virtual assistant is "an independent entrepreneur providing administrative, creative, and/or technical services. They work on a contractual basis from their own home or office. With companies becoming more global and transportable, the virtual assistant business is booming.

The concept of the virtual assistant fits in perfectly with the small business entrepreneur. For one thing, they are entrepreneurs themselves and will have a good understanding of what you want to accomplish. It's also a boon economically because of the savings in taxes, health insurance, vacation and sick pay, and other costs related to having a regular, full-time employee.

And, let's face it, time is money. In the beginning you will be able to handle it all yourself, but as soon as you have two, three, four, or more businesses up and running, there just simply won't be enough time in a day to do everything yourself.

According to the Small Business Administration "the average small business owner spends up to 40% of their time on routine administrative tasks". Virtual assistants take the administrative burden off of you, leaving you time to sell, market, do speaking engagements, and interviews.

I found my assistant through a personal recommendation, but you can easily find one by going online. Check out their website to see if it's professionally put together. Check for grammatical and spelling errors, writing skills, etc. You want to make sure her personality matches with yours and that she understands your business and your objectives.

HOW TO FIND A GOOD VIRTUAL ASSISTANT:

- Make sure they are on time and professional since they will be representing your business. Follow-through is also very important.
- Make sure they have the experience and skills you need for your particular business.
- Find a virtual assistant who has held an upper-level position in business.
- Find someone who is a confident self-starter. You will be way too busy to constantly hold their hand. You want someone you can trust to take charge and get things done.
- Get references and check out their testimonials, just as you would anyone else you are going to do business with.
- Ask for samples of their writing, graphics, or web work. Start with the smallest package of time until you figure out whether you will work well together or not.
- Make sure you are speaking the same language, especially with a virtual assistant you hire from another country. Sometimes things get lost in translation.
- Be clear about what you want, even with assistants in the U.S. If it's a complicated task or you want it done a certain way, spell it all out to avoid problems down the road.

FULFILLMENT

If you sell one or more products, having a fulfillment company working for you behind the scenes frees up a lot of your valuable time.

In the beginning I would recommend doing it yourself. But when you get to the point that you can make more money just selling instead of spending time hauling boxes to the post office, it's time to look into a fulfillment company. And you will also probably get tired of having boxes stacked in every corner of your house or apartment.

Bob Boylan of Xpert Fulfillment explains why you should use a fulfillment company:

Handled correctly, using a fulfillment company can reduce your order processing and warehousing costs, get you bigger shipping discounts, and cut back on employees.

PROS

- Focus on selling
- A good fulfillment company will reduce your expenses
- They understand shipping and can make suggestions that will save you money
- Save money on packaging because fulfillment companies purchase massive quantities of packaging
- No labor issues

CONS

- You will be giving up some control
- You will be depending on someone else to take care of the shipping.

How do you choose the right fulfillment partner?

Make sure you qualify them and they are responsive to your questions. Be sure to ask for a few references.

Provide them with a file of recent shipping activity. They should be able to provide you with details of what they would've charged you to ship those same packages.

They should be upfront about their pricing. There shouldn't be any hidden fees and you need to know what happens if your volume increases or drops.

How knowledgeable are the sales staff? How much do they know about what happens during package processing?

Are there packaging fees, receiving fees, storage fees? Do you need returns processing? What happens if an order is shipped incorrectly? How friendly is the order management software?

All fulfillment providers will warehouse your inventory and ship out your goods. However, all of them will handle and process your orders differently. It's how they differ that makes your decision so important. Don't always be scared off by the basic per order and per item numbers.

If a fulfillment company says that they use every carrier, then chances are that they have not negotiated great rates with all of them. More often than not, the carriers will negotiate with fulfillment service centers based on the percentage of business that the fulfillment company will give them.

Therefore chances are that a fulfillment center with a primary carrier will be able to give you a better discount because they have a large enough shipping margin to pass one on to you.

Be honest with the fulfillment companies that you are dealing with. The more detail you provide about your shipping habits, the more accurately they will be able to quote your rates.

It's important to consider their flexibility. You'll find that a smaller fulfillment service provider may be able to work much better with you than a larger corporate giant. The smaller companies are more concerned with the profit they can turn.

Ask things like "Who are your competitors?" This can be surprisingly revealing. Then ask "Why should I chose you over your competition?" Do they have a good response? Are they confident that they can serve you better than the competition?

Another factor to carefully consider when selecting your order fulfillment company is the physical location of their facility. In the world of shipping and logistics there are zones. Zones are basically an index of distance between the point of origin and the destination.

Carriers will charge different shipping rates depending on the zone. The point is to find a fulfillment house that is centrally located.

How creative are the fulfillment companies that you are having quote on your business? Do they care about your business goals and desire to help you get to that point. If they gouge you on fees and overcharge you on shipping it will limit you.

A good fulfillment company will make suggestions for helping you cut costs, and they will find ways to help you grow.

Ask about inventory check-in. This is commonly called "dock top shelf" time and it's the amount of time that goes by between when your goods arrive on the fulfillment company's dock and when they are checked in and ready to ship. Times can range from a few hours to a few days, so be sure to check what the average is.

Also ask about information reporting. What information is provided to you after an order is shipped? Can you get information on the Internet or do you have to call? Can you search for an order by name or by order number? Can you track packages to see if they've been delivered? The more information you have, the easier it will be to deal with inquiries.

PUT IT INTO ACTION

- [ ] Look for a virtual assistant
- [ ] Hire some college students to help you and get used to delegating
- [ ] Look online for distribution companies that would be a good fit for your product
- [ ] Write out a six and twelve month plan for using reps for your product

7

Crop Protection and Pest Management

"Business is a combination of war and sport."
—ANDRE MAUROIS

One violent hailstorm could devastate a crop and a whole economy overnight. A new high-tech device called a hail cannon switches on whenever a storm is approaching and literally turns damaging hail into non-threatening raindrops by emitting a deafening, electronic blast every six seconds. Unfortunately, every business needs its own hail cannon and pest management system. The United States has more lawyers per capita than any other country in the world and Americans spend more on civil litigation than any other industrialized country.

This isn't the most fun chapter, but I have learned the hard way that it's one of the most important. It's much better to be over-prepared than under-protected. Before you launch your business you need to make sure you have the best security in place. And you need to set this up in the beginning. Three things you need to secure first are legal, accounting, and insurance.

LEGAL

Understanding your legal risks is one of the most important things an entrepreneur can do. You need to be able to spot these issues before they become a bigger problem. That can be done by protecting yourself and your assets before your business gets off the ground. Do your homework and read up on some of the legal issues you'll be facing. A good place to start is NoLo.com. They have plenty of information and low-cost ways to get started.

From the standpoint of personal liability alone, you should incorporate your business. A corporation may enter into contracts, sue and be sued, and own property. And it offers the advantage of limited liability, meaning your *personal* assets (house, car, etc.) can be kept separate from the business.

Before you decide on which form of organization you want to go with, you should seek the advice of a good CPA. Because laws differ from state to state, you want to pick the best business form to suit your needs. There are advantages and drawbacks to each one.

Find a good business attorney and do everything right from the beginning. If you're filing for a patent, get a patent attorney. Make sure your trademarks and copyrights are solidly protected.

There are inexpensive prepaid legal services (easy to find through Google) which may be able to help with things like reviewing simple business contracts, dealing with leases and creditors, and writing cease and desist letters if necessary. This will save you money. But whatever you do, always, always have an attorney read over every contract you sign. Not doing so is a mistake that only needs to be made once. Trust me. Now I rarely sign contracts over two pages long, and I prefer that it be written in plain English. Make sure you always understand what you're signing and don't rush it, *no matter what.* No contract needs to be signed at midnight on a napkin. (I'm just saying.)

Living in Los Angeles, I thought finding an attorney would be a piece of cake. You could probably throw a rock and hit ten of them. But when the time came for me to get one, I couldn't believe how hard it was. Especially to find the right one.

One of the first places to look is through referrals. A friend who has worked with an attorney will know more about them. But even so, you want to make sure they are the right attorney for the job.

This is another hard lesson that I learned. Just because someone is a great tax attorney, don't assume they know anything about patents. Find someone who specializes in exactly what you need. It's best to find an attorney who understands your specific industry and the jargon that is used.

An attorney who has worked with business owners before may also have connections and networking leads such as accountants and bankers.

Attorney billing:

- Make sure the attorney is ethical and won't over bill you. Let them know what your budget is up front, and put it in writing that you will be notified if the bill is up to the limit of the retainer you put down.
- You can and should also put in writing how you want to be billed and what items you will and won't pay for. You should also demand monthly billing. Never allow too much time to go by.
- Get them to quote you a price up front. Granted, things can sometimes take longer than expected, but at least get a quote that is as close as possible.
- Though attorneys usually charge by the hour, you can often arrange to pay a flat fee for things like registering a trademark or drafting a contract.
- Because attorneys are always on the clock, prepare as much as possible before you speak to them so you don't waste time.
- Make sure your attorney is on your side and understands what you are trying to accomplish. Make sure he or she understands your financial situation and have them explain up front what things cost.

Even if the attorney comes from a referral, look them up on Martindale.com and find out where they went to school. See if they have any negative reviews from past clients or have been reprimanded by the bar.

Once you have your corporation, make sure you file the appropriate paperwork to avoid paying unnecessary fines and fees. Reevaluate your business entity from time to time. You can change it if you need to as your business grows.

Get a business license and any other permits you will need. Almost all businesses require a county or city license. This gives you the privilege of operating a business within your jurisdiction. Your business could be considered a low, moderate, or high impact business.

Low impact would be a low noise level, few to no customers on the premises, and high impact businesses usually wouldn't be allowed in a residential area because of the noise and traffic. You need to contact local authorities to find out which permits you'll need.

Some businesses require special licensing and some require written or oral examinations. Some examples would be massage, hairdressing, plumbing, pest control, etc. Real estate agencies and insurance agencies require occupational permits. Make sure you check before you start your business. Some businesses require a federal license. This would include businesses that are highly regulated by the government.

Businesses that sell products to the public usually collect a sales tax. I learned this the hard way in my first year of business. I got a huge tax bill from the state because I didn't take care of it, and they put down that I sold $300,000 worth of products, which was about $290,000 off the mark. When I asked where they got that number, they said they just made it up. Lesson to be learned . . . take care of things before the government starts pulling numbers out of a hat.

ACCOUNTING

A good small business accountant should do more than just file your taxes. They can be someone who helps you grow your business, and not just a number cruncher. A certified public accountant usually charges more, but it can be worth it, as they will help you with more than just your taxes. They should double as a general business consultant who can offer advice on things like risk management, pricing, and inventory control.

The Society of Certified Public Accountants suggests asking these questions before choosing a CPA:

- How long has your firm been in business? Some clients want a more established CPA, while others want one with a smaller client list for more personal attention.
- Do you offer an initial consultation and is there a charge? Many firms offer a free initial consultation.
- Can I contact any of your current clients for a referral? A reputable firm will be willing to provide these.
- What education have you recently completed in your area of expertise? CPAs who have an active certificate to practice public accounting are required to complete a certain amount of continuing education.
- What computer programs do you prefer your clients use for record keeping? They should be able to help you set up and maintain computerized bookkeeping.

It's a good idea to start your business off on the right track from the beginning. My first inventory control was just a mess. I would fall behind in my accounting, so I never knew how much inventory I actually had. You can avoid this pitfall by establishing a relationship with an accountant early in the process.

A good benefit of being your own boss and having a home business is the many tax breaks. A portion of your mortgage or rent can be tax deductible. So are your business phone calls and office equipment. A portion of any direct expenses, such as utilities, insurance, and repairs may also be tax deductible.

INSURANCE

Having the right kind of insurance for your business gives you peace of mind and financial protection in case of an accident or anything else that might hit you out of left-field.

Here are some examples of different types of coverage:

- Health and medical coverage
- Property coverage
- Liability coverage
- Directors and officers coverage
- Disability coverage

Health and medical coverage:

In the beginning, you may only have insurance for yourself, but as you grow and take on employees, you'll probably want to look into group health insurance.

The process of securing small business health insurance can be tedious but worth it. In some states you only need one employee, and some states require that you have at least two employees.

Benefits include spreading the financial risk between all members, which means lower premiums and better coverage for everyone.

Property insurance:

Property insurance covers damage or loss to your business property, including inventory, office furniture and supplies, and equipment.

Different policies have different coverage limits. Special form coverage provides the most protection.

Liability insurance:

A general liability policy can cover things like slip and fall accidents on your property.

Product liability insurance protects you from lawsuits by customers who claim to be injured by your product. Usually large retailers will require that you have this before they will put the product in their stores.

Directors and officers coverage:

This type of insurance covers directors and officers of your company in case of a lawsuit as it relates to their performance with the company. This can usually include Employment Practices Liability, which involves harassment and discrimination suits.

You will usually be required to have Directors and Officers Liability Insurance when you have a board of directors. Investors will also require that you have this before they will consider funding your company. Directors will want protection against claims from employees, clients, and stockholders so that they won't be personally held responsible.

Disability coverage:

If you can't live without your current income, you should seriously consider purchasing disability insurance. If you're self-employed, you'll be responsible for your own, but it could really come in handy.

Here are the facts:

One third of all Americans between the ages of 35 and 65 will become disabled for more than 90 days, according to the American Council of Life Insurers. One in seven will be disabled for more than five years. This could be due to accidents or illness and can drive some people to the brink of bankruptcy.

Disability insurance plans vary, but none of them will pay you 100% of your income. You need to decide how much you can live on and whether you need to go for the maximum or not.

COPYRIGHT, TRADEMARK, AND PATENT INFRINGEMENT PROTECTION

They say that imitation is the sincerest form of flattery. But don't tell that to anyone who has had their copyrights, trademarks, or patents infringed. For anyone who has labored over a project just to have it stolen out from under them, I can tell you that the first time you find an infringer it's not only hurtful, it's infuriating.

The first time I saw an infringer I couldn't believe it. Not only did they steal my patents, trademarks, and copyrights, but they used my picture on their website! I bookmarked the site for future reference because using someone's pictures and copy without their permission is a violation of copyright law and I wanted to keep the proof.

I started checking my product on a regular basis and even more infringers came out of the woodwork. I had my attorney draft up a cease and desist letter to send to the infringers (who were all in China, by the way). The letter was basically ignored by all of them. So I started calling and emailing them one by one.

I contacted the directories where they were advertising. They all have an intellectual property form at the bottom of the page. I made several copies of them and just kept filling them out and faxing. As soon as one infringer came down off of the site, another one took their place.

I also sent everything in my file to the search engines to have them taken off of the Internet, which takes a very, very long time. Just as Google Alerts are great to monitor any news stories that come out about your products, Google Alerts is also a good way to find out who is infringing on your copyrights, trademarks, and patents. Google your product and similar keywords every week to keep an eye out for unauthorized activity related to your product. Don't just look under your brand name. They will get tricky and change the description. Also look through other search engines and foreign search engines as well.

A lot of the directories have a product alert feature. Ask to be put on their alert email for your item. That's a good way to find out instantly if someone is violating your patents and trademarks.

Go to the companies that are hosting the infringers and ask them to remove them. Be prepared to give them your patent and trademark information. Register your product with the International Trade Commission, which monitors all of the major ports, to prevent inventory from coming into the country that violates your rights. Contact the International Chamber of Commerce, which is a non-profit organization that promotes global trade.

As a last resort, there are attorneys who will work on patent and trademark infringement on a contingency basis. If you're not successful in stopping them from selling your product, get an attorney to go after them for damages.

I started a blog called infringerblacklist.com because I was so exasperated with the tactics of infringers. After putting many years of my life into something just to have someone steal it . . . uh, uh. That is NOT okay. Also, I searched everywhere for information on infringement and didn't find a whole lot. I figured there were others out there who were looking for the same thing and were frustrated at the system.

So, I created one more Money Garden business because of a problem that needed to be fixed. It put me on a crusade. I'm now helping other businesses get rid of infringers and getting paid for it. If you feel passionate about something and can help others, make a business out of it. Turn your passion into profit.

The lesson here is that every business is going to run into problems sooner or later, so use the information in this chapter to protect yourself as much as possible. And—always be aware of the possibility of turning a problem into an opportunity.

EXIT STRATEGY

An exit strategy in business is important and should be considered in the beginning. It may be many years down the road, but it's never too early to start planning how you will wind down your business.

There's more than one way to exit a business including an initial public offering (IPO), sale to a family member, or an acquisition by a larger company.

You've worked hard to build your business and you should get as much out of it as you can. This takes careful planning.

John Leonetti, founder and managing director of Pinnacle Equity Solutions, an exit strategy planning firm, takes us through his 6-step process for business owners who want to prepare their best exit strategy:

PART I: Preparing For Your Exit

Step 1: Establish your exit goals

The process for setting an exit strategy plan begins with your goals. However, it is equally important to know where you currently are. There are both financial and mental obstacles that need to be examined to design your optimal exit.

Step 2: Personal readiness to exit

Financial readiness

If you are like most business owners today, you are depending upon the proceeds from your exit to satisfy your lifestyle after leaving the business. You need to know the amount of investable assets that will satisfy your financial goals. Forecast your pre and post-exit expenses and measure your personal lifestyle to score your financial readiness as either high or low.

Mental readiness

You need to know what the business really means to you—personally—and what you are going to do with your time after the business exit. The key indicator of this mental readiness is usually how involved you are in the day-to-day operations of the business.

   Are you really ready to leave your business? You will rank this readiness as high or low.

Step 3: Identify the type of exiting owner you most resemble

There are four general types of exiting owners. Your financial readiness and your mental readiness will tell you what type of exiting owner you most resemble. This examination then leads you towards identifying the exit options that are most likely suitable for you to begin to build your exit strategy plan.

PART II: Knowing Your Options

Step 4: Learn and choose your optimal exit option

A complete exit strategy will examine all exit options available to determine which one is the best fit for helping you achieve your overall goals. This may include:

1. A sale of the business to an outside party
2. A private equity group recapitalization
3. An employee stock ownership plan
4. Management buyout
5. A gifting program

Or any combination of these or other options. The book explains each of these exit options and illustrates them through case studies.

Step 5: Understanding the value of the option you choose

Each exit option has a different value associated with it. For example, an internal transfer to an employee stock ownership plan is measured at fair market value, while a sale to an outside party is measured at market, or synergy value.

In order to examine the outcome from analyzing each of the options, you need to know something about the "Range of Values" that exists for your privately-held business. You will learn the valuation that is relevant to each exit option and what tools can be used to figure out the net result that will be achieved from each exit.

PART III: Planning Your Exit, Protecting Your Wealth

Step 6: Execute your exit strategy plan to achieve your exit goals and to protect your illiquid business wealth

Execution of your exit strategy plan will include coordination and planning involving deal structuring, taxes, estate planning, legal agreements, and much more.

Being sure that you have a competent and professional advisory team in place is essential for a smooth and successful exit.

"Exiting Your Business, Protecting Your Wealth" can be found on Pinnacle's website at www.exitingyourbusiness.com.

PUT IT INTO ACTION

- ☐ Find a good attorney through a referral and make sure you check them out
- ☐ Find a good accountant who can also help you run your business
- ☐ Protect your intellectual property in every way you can
- ☐ Register your trademarks with the International Trade Commission
- ☐ Set up Google alerts to find infringers
- ☐ Look through the search engines every week to monitor your intellectual property
- ☐ List the three biggest problems facing you now, and brainstorm ways to turn them into opportunities

Reaping What You Sow
The Check's in the Mail

For anyone who's ever planted a real garden, you know how exciting it is to see the first sprouts start to grow. You've labored over the tilling and seeding and watering, and you've been patient for a long time. Now you begin to see the actual fruits of your labor paying off.

This is exactly what will happen with your Money Garden. In the beginning, you'll work hard and plant seeds everywhere, and expect them to pay off right away. I know, we live in a fast-paced world with sound bites and fast food. We want it immediately and we don't want to wait for it.

A Money Garden is a work in progress. You'll start to see income rather quickly, but it'll take a while to grow to the point that you can make a great living with it. Don't give up. Keep working on it every single day, and believe me, one day you will open your mailbox or your PayPal account and the big check will be there. I've seen it happen. The most I've made so far is $20,000 in one day. It's a great feeling.

It's also a great feeling to get emails and letters from people all over the world who have used and enjoyed your products. I've gotten some from countries I've never even heard of.

I hope you enjoyed reading this book as much as I enjoyed writing it. I would love to hear about your progress, your successes, and your setbacks. Also, let me know if there are areas where you would like more information.

Check back often at www.createforcash.com for new books and products.

You can reach me at createforcash@gmail.com.

Best of luck!
Julie

www.ingramcontent.com/pod-product-compliance
Lightning Source LLC
Chambersburg PA
CBHW070351200326
41518CB00012B/2210